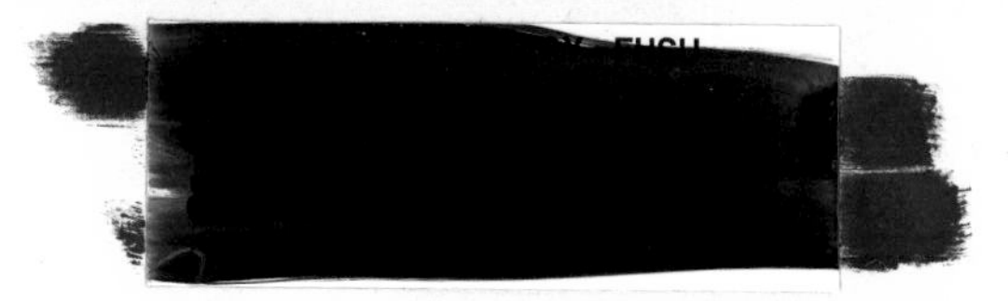

GIVE OR TAKE A CENTURY

An Eskimo Chronicle

Joseph Engasongwok Senungetuk

A Self-Portrait, 1970

Joseph E. Senungetuk

GIVE OR TAKE A CENTURY

An Eskimo Chronicle

The Indian Historian Press
San Francisco

A MODERN PUBLISHING CLASSIC BY

The Indian Historian Press, Inc.

Native American Educational Publishers

Library of Congress Catalog Card Number 73-141290

Printed in the United States of America.

To Jeannette and Rupert, without whom this book would not be possible. To Jan, for her wifely encouragement; and to Jennifer and her grandparents.

J.E.S.

The Chapter head illustration: This drawing is from an ivory carving found in an Ipiutak burial site at Point Hope, Alaska. It shows the skeletal motif widely used by Eskimo artists during pre-white contact days. The Ipiutak culture is believed to have existed until about 200 B.C. The motif greatly resembles the decorations of carved objects done in the Scytho-Siberian style of the region between the Black Sea and the Ordos area of Northern China (900 to 200 B.C.).

Drawings, illustrations, and
all art work by the author,
Joseph Engasongwok Senungetuk.

Introduction

Native people whose land and cultures have been overrun by an alien society suffer more than the loss of a homeland. They bear the less visible but more profound loss of the ancient historic memory. Their remembrance of a specific history, which was cherished by the elders and handed on from generation to generation as part of a rich and noble heritage, is damaged. Only with great effort is the historic knowledge recaptured. It takes a "reaching back" into time and space, behind the alien culture, to find one's place again in the home of the original native culture. This is especially true in America, where the truth is so often buried under conventional but false notions of how this nation began her passage to the dominant place she now has in history.

The story of Alaska and her peoples is a case in point. A considerable amount of research material is now available concerning Eskimo and Indian cultures. However, the Native himself, subject of the research, has lost much of the personal knowledge about his own lifeways and history.

And so this book is for the Natives, my own people, as well as for the foreigners who now dwell among us.

There are other, more palpable results of the foreign intrusion. These results involve the decimation of whole populations, the introduction of new and violent diseases, the kind of poverty from which the Native cannot extricate himself by his efforts alone, the destruction of Native technology, the expropriation of land and appropriation of natural resources for the sole purpose of profits, the failure to provide education, and the systematic evisceration of our important well established culture together with our languages.

The effect upon the Native is a tragedy of massive proportions. Our travail is not yet ended. The expropriation of our land and resources continues. The results of promises are slender and shadowy, lacking substance. More and more chapters are being added to this tragic story, in a time when understanding and humanity are found in meagre quantities, as the exception rather than as a law of nature.

We who are the Natives of this land are sick with waiting for the changes and improvements that have been promised us. We have been patient. We can be patient still. Just the same, we ask:

Give or take a century . . . how much longer must we wait!

Contents

CHAPTER	PAGE
1. Two Worlds Meet	1
2. The Innupiat	9
3. Kingetkin: Village of Wales	15
4. Land and Language	26
5. Village and Family	39
6. The Seal Hunt	50
7. Climate and Food	65
8. Our World in Transition	73
9. Eh Sah Ne: Taboo	82
10. The Hunter	89
11. To Nome	106
12. Departure by Bush Plane	113

13. "Strange Noises" in Nome 119

14. An Eskimo Family in Nome 129

15. Struggle for Survival 138

16. Civilization and Its Problems 159

17. The Old and the New 166

18. The Hide Box 175

Chronology of Alaskan Native History 182

Inventions and Contributions 200

Native Organizations 203

Names You Should Know 205

1

Two Worlds Meet

The landing of foreigners on Alaskan soil first came about on what is now Southeastern Alaska. Like ants scurrying away from their homes, zigzagging hither and yonder, leaving with the traded furs and Native artifacts, and returning for more of the loot, these adventurers came from countries as varied as Spain, Portugal, Denmark, Germany and Russia.

The earliest recorded year for such foreign contact with the Native in Alaska occurred in 1582, when some nondescript characters from Macao in Southeast China are said to have accidentally landed on the shores of the Tlingit country. They were commissioned by the King of Spain to find a passage to Asia.

Occupying the coasts and inland areas of Alaska at this time were many tribes, such as the Tlingit Indians, Ingalik, Koyukon, Kutchin, Tanana, the Aleuts and the Eskimo. After two centuries of such meandering by hopeful sailors, the Dane, Vitus Bering, entered the picture. His Kamchatka expeditions, undertaken by order of Czar Peter the Great, were failures. He met with unexpectedly powerful currents and foul weather. Upon his third attempt, in 1741, he was more successful. On June 15th of that year he left the coast of Kamchatka in the ship St. Peter, a second ship following, the St. Paul. On July 26th, the St. Paul, separated from the St. Peter due to a storm, landed on the American coast. Captain Chirikof sent in twenty of his men to reconnoiter. They never returned. He saw a canoe full of Natives, but since he had no other boat for landing purposes, he sailed back to Kamchatka.

On July 19, 1741, Vitus Bering landed near what is now known as Yakutat Bay. On August 1st he sailed back to what he thought was the route home, making port at some of the islands along the way, but never for long. Finally land was spotted, which he mistook for Kamchatka. It was actually what is now Bering Island. He was to die of illness there after his anchored ship was wrecked on the rocks. His crew survived on water mammals, and built a boat from the wreckage of their ship. They returned home the following year.

Thereafter the Aleutian Islands became the slaughtering yards for Russian exploiters who were known as "promyschlenniks," (entreprenneurs, industrialists). Their greed and brutality was matched only by the gold-struck Americans a century and a half later. The Russians spent intervals of two to three years raising havoc with the land and products of the sea, and left a heritage of foreign diseases with the Natives — the Aleuts, Koniags, and South Central Alaskan Eskimos. In 1761 the Russians began to winter on the mainland.

From the south, even before the Tlingits felt the full force of the Russian fur traders, came explorers from other nations. Particularly were the Spanish interested, who made haste to sail northward to find out what the Russians were so excited about. Juan Perez, in 1774, reached the northern tip of the Queen Charlotte Islands. The next year, more Spanish expeditions were sent north from California. Some were astonished to find belligerent Natives who paid no attention to their "This-land-is-my-land" ceremonies. They were surrounded by Natives in Sitka, and then were forced to pay for their food supplies and water, which they had to procure themselves.

In 1778, Captain Cook entered the scene of this epic, in which two worlds met and clashed — the Old and the New. He was looking for a northerly passage to the Atlantic Ocean. He was killed in 1779 by a Sandwich Islander. His successor, working up the Bering Strait, fell ill and died shortly thereafter. The crew headed home without going further. They landed in China, selling for high prices the furs they had acquired from the Alaska Natives in exchange for worthless trinkets. Back home in England they told of the fantastic profits. Trading companies were hastily formed, not only in England, but in the young United States, China, India, and many European countries.

Ten years later, other trading parties began to see a dwindling of the Native population, the adults' faces pockmarked, their distrust of the European interlopers mounting. Reports soon appeared accusing the Spaniards of introducing smallpox, and practicing various types of mistreatment against the Natives. Competition, bickering, profiteering now developed between the exploiting countries. Prices of furs rose and fell. An oversupply in Asia brought about new trade with Europe. Soon the Natives began to evaluate the trustworthiness of certain companies or ships. Weapons traded for furs gave some avaricious captains reason to become wary. Encounters of the foreign adventurers with the Natives brought bloodshed, and the supply diminished, particularly of the fur-bearing animals such as the fur seal and the sea otter. Soon Russia was the only nation left with plans for futher expansion of the animal-slaughter enterprise, particularly in the less-traded areas.

In 1790, Alexander Baranof became the head of Russia's American possessions. He went to the mainland and established peaceful relations with the Natives, mainly by showmanship, many promises, and a gift made of copper: the Russian royal crest, and a picture of the heir to the Russian throne.

Five years later, this uneasy peace was shattered, and there were battles with the various Indian clans and tribes along the way to Yakutat Bay. Planting the Russian flag and the crest of the Russian empire on Alaskan soil, Baranof had laid claim to the coastline. Through the Baranof & Shelikof Company, the Aleuts were forced to be baptized into the Greek Catholic faith and were conscripted for a three-year term of service to the company. Shelikof died, and the new Russian-America Company was formed. In 1779, Baranof, seeking more power, sailed to Sitka Bay to establish new fur factories. He took along the Aleut conscripts. But at Sitka, he was met by three hundred distrustful Natives. Again the world of Russian diplomacy, reinforced by superior weaponry, and brutality, won the day, and construction of the Sitka factory was begun.

When the factory was completed, Baranof returned to the Kodiak headquarters. Six hundred Tlingit Indians invaded the new Russian exploiting branch at Sitka, and demolished the fort which was a part of the industrial enterprise. Afterwards, other Russian forts were tested for their security by other Native tribes. Baranof felt he had to stop these attacks. He began to ravage the coastline, taking fur pelts by the thousands and destroying two Indian villages, Kake and Kujus.

A full scale war was then planned against the Sitka Indians, and Baranof deployed four large ships to Sitka Sound on September 19, 1804. Three hundred and fifty baidarkas (Aleut skin boats), were also sent in. Fifty of them were lost during the stormy journey from Kodiak to Sitka.

By this time Baranof had become known to the Native villagers as a vengeful man. All along the coast, smaller villages heard of his coming and fled for their lives. Only in Sitka did he find the Natives ready to fight. On September 29, 1804, the Tlingits offered to negotiate and sent their messenger to the Russian bastion. No agreement was reached. The Sitka Tlingits insisted that no fort should be established.

On October 1st, Baranof attacked the Tlingits situated near the Indian River. His attack was unsuccessful, and his Aleut conscripts deserted him. Retreat to the ships was now the only recourse, and Baranof was wounded during the retreat.

The master of a second ship took over operations then, utilizing all the cannon and rifle fire available, and the Tlingits asked for peace talks. Aleut prisoners captured earlier by the Tlingits were to be released; hostages were to be given to the Russians. Lisiansky, Russian member of the expeditionary force, took charge of the Aleut prisoners and the hostages. Information reached him that the Tlingits had sent for reinforcements, however. He considered this to be evidence of new plans for resuming hostilities. Six days later, shots were fired upon the Tlingits from the ships. On October 7th, 1804, ravens were seen circling above the fort, and it was discovered the Tlingits had left, except for two old women and a boy. Baranof razed the fort and began to build another factory on New Archangel Hill.

The following year the Tlingits regrouped at Chatham Strait north of Sitka, and Baranof invited them to discuss peace terms. Ceremonies in the Tlingit tradition were now observed by Baranof in regal style. Kotlian, the Tlingit leader, agreed to come to his original home area to talk with the Russians, who had so ignominiously expropriated his hunting and fishing grounds. Forced to give up his settlement in Sitka, the Indian leader had already built a fortress at Chatham Strait, with a population numbering between 1,300 and 1,400.

Kotlian's preparations for defense of his homeland gave the other tribes courage to mount a struggle for their land, even when it became clear they would have to fight their neighboring tribes. The Yakutat Indians were all but wiped out by the Chugach (an Eskimo clan), when a Russian settlement leader, Uvarof, pitted the two tribes against each other.

When the Kodiak base learned of the fall of the Yakutats, 200 Aleuts, en route to Kodiak from Sitka, were deployed to Yakutat Bay to retaliate. In an extremely rough storm, they were all but wiped out. Historians call this a "loss" for the Russians — no loss for the Aleuts themselves!

With more bribery, and more cajoling, the Russian leaders at New Archangel were now able to appease the angry Tlingit chiefs. Feasts were arranged, where the Indians were honored by the so-called ambassadors of the Czar.

In 1808, Baranof decided to move his seat of administrative operations to a new Archangel at Sitka. This man has been lauded by contemporaries and historians, as a great leader and an efficient manager for the fur companies. In the next three to eight years, having lost his old energy, he asked repeatedly for retirement, and finally died in 1819 at Batavia, at the age of 72.

Baranof's successors made contracts with the promyschlenniks, and rubles were exchanged in the hundreds of thousands. The only compensation received by the original Native inhabitants was strict military discipline, protection if the whites deemed their behavior to be cooperative, and permission to build some fishing camps. By this time, however, the Tlingits had learned how to exact hard trading bargains, and they did so with the new French companies. Liquor and rifles began to make their way into the trading circles.

In 1867, the United States bought the Russian territory of Alaska for $7,200,000. This occurred after the Russian Crown realized it was dealing with a troublesome Native people, and had just taken over administration of the fur trading companies. In all these transactions, the Natives received no consideration whatever.

The Americans now laid eager hands upon the land of the Indians, Aleuts and Eskimos. Canneries were established in Alaska; gold was discovered; Native women were abused. The pinch of want began to be felt, and the introduction of the dollar pitted all factions against each other. The resultant "sins" were "discovered" by the churches, and missionaries arrived, to add still another flavor to an era in which the Tragedy of Alaska came to its most profound infamy. Certainly the depredations committed by the foreigners upon a great country and its inhabitants have made it most difficult, if not impossible, to reinstate this land as one in which Native man proved his unique ability to co-exist with the earth and its treasures.

Contrary to popular belief, the three peoples who made up the Alaskan population prior to foreign intervention, are not of the same stock. The Eskimo constitute a distinct race, with their many clans and tribes and varied dialects. So do the Aleuts. The Indians also, in their many and varied tribes, constitute another Native racial group. The results of such foreign intrusion upon their lands were tragic. The Aleuts, who were located on the Aleutian Islands, Shumagin Islands, and the western part of the Alaskan peninsula, are believed to have had a population of approximately 25,000 before arrival of the foreigners in 1741. Brutally treated by the Russians, they were soon reduced to one-tenth of their population, and in 1848 were reported to have not more than 900 persons left. During the second World War, in the early 1940's Japanese military personnel invaded Attu, one of the Aleutian Islands, thus paying back in their own coin the Americans and Russians who laid greedy hands upon the Aleut land in years past.

The Tlingits, who occupied land in Southeastern Alaska and along the Canadian line, fought and died. Their numbers also vastly declined as a result of diseases, superior weaponry, and crushing economic impoverishment.

The foreigners made contact with the Eskimo people at a later date, due to the relative inaccessibility of most Eskimo villages. In my own country, Wales, we were reached by whaling ships into Point Barrow, the Diomede Islands and Wales. We too felt the harsh fist of this intrusion, diseases being primarily responsible for the decimation of the people.

The tragedy of Alaska is an epic story still untold. It is with the Eskimo of this land that I am mainly concerned in this book, and particularly with my own people, the Eskimo of Northwestern Alaska at Wales.

ANCIENT ART – USE UNKNOWN

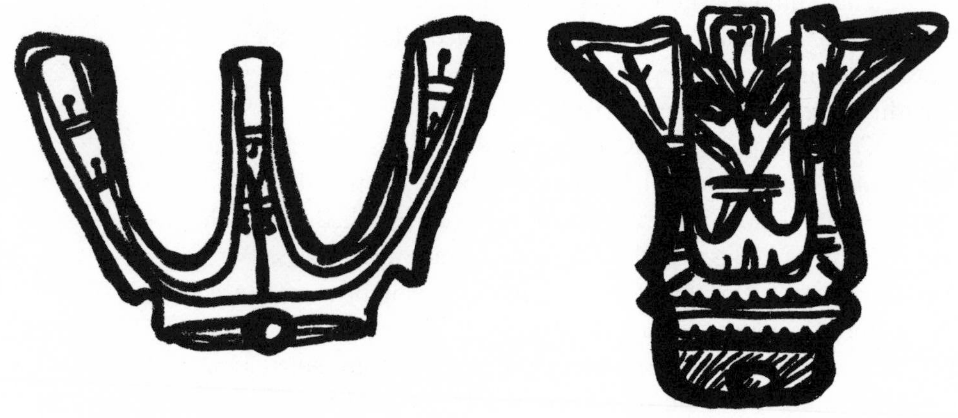

Tridents. Both are from three to seven inches across, and both have holes through midcenter bottom, and midcenter top.

Butterfly shapes. (These objects shown on the page were found in ancient Alaskan sites. Their uses, whether ornamental or utilitarian are still unknown.)

2

The Innupiat

There are many Eskimos still living in Alaska today. They call themselves "Innupiat," which means "the real people." I am one of these people. But, whatever I have read about the Eskimo has been inaccurate. There is much to learn about my ancestors, but I feel that the usual "authoritative" sources do not offer this knowledge.

I know that during my childhood years I was living in a world offering both sides of the cultural picture. Too, all during those early years I was being prepared for a way of life totally different from that of my parents. Such a stage of society, in such a world, can best be described as "transitional," and the Eskimo in transition is our particular pre-occupation in this book. Ancient beliefs and traditions blend with the new, and blending, make up a different social and cultural situation. Too often is the life of the people before white contact considered as static, unchanging, all of one piece. This is historically inaccurate. It is certainly an inaccurate way of looking at the story of man as he lived and died and lived again through the thousands of years he has spent upon this earth. The Eskimo peoples, just as all others, knew change throughout their history . . . change that took place slowly to be sure, but before white contact involved the slow and painstaking development of specific technology, the use but not the exploitation of land and sea, as well as changes in social relationships and economy. Thus, while my preoccupation is with my own people at a particular stage of their development, when the European-Native cultural clash was well under way, the ancient life is as much a part of the story as if I had myself lived it with all my heart and being.

Willie Senungetuk, my father, has lived much of his life in Wales, Alaska. This small spot in Northwestern Alaska is my own birthplace. He has fathered one daughter and three sons. The greatest part of his life took place during an extraordinary time in Alaskan history, when missionaries, schoolteachers, traders, miners, military men, and mercenary adventurers were ending a period during which they had completely overwhelmed the native culture. My own grandparents enjoyed their ancient, satisfying, steadfast way of life. But they did not live to see their children's heartbreaking struggles in adjusting their lives and beliefs to a totally different culture. My parents managed to make some sort of uneasy peace with the white culture, but not without damage. In turn, my own life has been altogether different, in my relationships with the dominant culture, from that of both my parents and my grandparents.

The history of the Willie Senungetuk family, I feel, can apply to many of the Northwest Alaskan Eskimo family groups. Certainly the hardships endured by the elder folks are altogether too familiar. These hardships include uncertainties due to the choices available, as to which cultural standards to uphold and which to reject, the separation of village, family, and individuals. Our family was no exception to the hazards of what Western man calls "necessary acculturation," in a frontiersman's arena. I believe that something needs to be said about my own experience, so that more accurate information can be acquired about the Eskimos of Alaska, than what is available in school books and popular tracts today. This material has brought about an altogether false image of Eskimos and Eskimo life. These inaccurate ideas are held by virtually all American people, including those in the larger cities of Alaska. A stereotypic image has been created, in which the Eskimo is seen as a short, stocky Mongoloid, with a broad face, chewing on blubber, and living in an ice house. His most notable social customs are nearly always described as nose-rubbing and wife-swapping. To read books of this sort is to add insult to injustice against a once stalwart, proud race, living only for happiness and peace, in a remote land area which they knew and loved.

I do not pretend to be an anthropological expert about my people, and I do not wish to belittle the interest which has been shown by those few who have attempted to rectify what has been badly mishandled by others. I want only to introduce a small contribution, so that some understanding can emerge as to what it is like from the other side of the horizon.

Nor do I have a family tree or ancestral crest which can be traced back in time, or neatly filed as to position in society, political influence, or wealth in goods or money. Naturally there are no bits and pieces of paper, giving names, dates, and social position of great-grandparents and great-great-grandparents. Eskimo history is a part of a magnificent oral literature, and I can only know what is in my heart and spirit, and in the far reaches of my mind. I can only feel the strength of those ties that bind me to the deepest past of my people. Those things that are known to me as beliefs, knowledge of the land and sea, understanding of the ways of animals, and the love for the tongue of the Innupiat, are a simple part of my nature. I am always surprised that researchers consider these matters of some significance in their work.

Our family today consists of my father's brothers, himself, our mother, their children, his brother's children, and the grandchildren. This is as far as a personal knowledge of my family's immediate ancestry goes. There are some important reasons for this common lack of familiarity with precise Eskimo family background. One is that the early Eskimo families practiced the teaching of individual importance rather than "blood line." Another has to do with the results of imported diseases that invaded the villages of healthy Eskimo families. Imagine an onslaught of unknown diseases brought by invaders from another planet, infecting a whole population on earth. Then imagine a people decimated, harassed, deprived of any means of self-defense, left to poverty and sickness for more than a century. This was the Eskimo condition following white intrusion. Only now are the people beginning to recover from the effects of the foreigners' diseases and the clash of a foreign culture.

My grandparents may have been part of a communal society, without the implications or forms of government attributed to such types of governments today. They had no use for the standards of present-day societies, which rely upon dollars and monopolistic ownership. Rather, the direct relationship with nature, and practical experience passed on from generation to generation, upheld their social structure, without power struggles, wars, and political in-fighting. Surely my forefathers endured hardships. But the hardships were those dealing directly with nature. Such hardships are entirely different from the frustrations experienced by present day young Eskimos, torn by conflicting opinions as to which culture to recognize as reliable for one's survival.

My paternal grandparents died soon after my father reached adolescence, along with two younger brothers. My mother's parents died while she was still an infant, victims of the influenza epidemic which left the small village of Wales in a state of disaster. So many died as a result of this disease of the invaders, that the only recourse left was to dig a large burial pit at the cemetery, instead of individual graves.

From this time on, my parents' future was bleak. Even more hardships were heaped upon the few who survived. My father was separated from his two brothers, when different foster-parents adopted them, with legal name changes. In fact, the missionaries who recorded the names of the three brothers, entered their personal Eskimo names for the family name. My mother was taken to a distant relative. With all this destruction of families, turmoil and death, it is difficult to say how much I can relate as factual events. In describing the authentic life styles of the Eskimo family in Wales, I depend upon my knowledge of the paternal grandparents. Hence, I shall dwell more upon the general aspects of life, derived from my childhood years in Wales, listening to the recollections of my parents, relatives, and other Wales villagers. For me personally, there is also an impelling desire to help rid the literature of current inaccuracies and foolish clichés.

In the past, the geographical area of Alaska upon which Wales is situated was not one readily accessible to encroachment by early European explorers. Even today, the village site is a formidable expanse of coastal lowlands surrounded by rocky hills, with a commanding view of the Bering Strait due west. Located on the westernmost tip of the Seward Peninsula, it still has a population of a hundred and fifty Eskimos, the number of people counted after the influenza epidemic brought to us by the Europeans. Undoubtedly the population was greater before this tragedy, and such changes as occurred besides the sheer reduction in numbers of people, were most likely of the kind that my father's and mother's families experienced. The greater set-backs were those of the small community's loss of tranquility and efficiency, originally possessed by the larger, well-coordinated settlement. This larger village, with its unique governmental stability, evolved through centuries of developing and perfecting a culture especially adapted to the Wales terrain, climate, and food sources. Results of the influenza epidemic and the introduction of new diseases, the moving away of families to seek employment or education in mining towns and cities, have kept Wales from returning to its original population. The separation of families, destruction of family ties, and the resultant decrease of the labor force so essential in retaining traditional customs, have been instrumental in making yesteryear's village societies the breeding grounds for today's inept and ruinous semi-literate, semi-industrial towns of Northwestern Alaska.

Today, Wales is a unique type of settlement, with just a touch of the white culture, one of the few places on earth where Western civilization is not the primary concern of the inhabitants. (I might add, this is so at this time of writing. Conditions may change drastically.) There still lingers the generations-old feeling of unity and harmony among those who have chosen to stay, however. Perhaps it is no longer a legitimate last frontier for the United States, but it is nevertheless one which consists of people not ready nor willing to take the leap to a technologically-directed modern world. Things experienced in an average "Middletown, U.S.A." have not yet intruded into the realities of living in Wales. It would probably appear to be as strange a country to the tourist as any one of the numerous foreign countries fawned over by United States foreign aid agencies. As in many isolated villages in Alaska, the high cost of transportation deters those who may be interested in acquiring a basic knowledge of Northwestern Alaska. The natural resources of the state itself were relatively unexploited for the same reason, although this is subject to change because of the potentially profit-producing qualities of Alaska's oil. The more precise ethnological studies were done during the latter part of the 19th century and the early 20th century. Moreover, early reports were generally done by Scandinavians who made contact with the Canadian Eskimos some centuries before. The term "Eskimo" came to be descriptive not only of the tribes populating parts of Canada, but of the Eskimo people of Alaska as well. The Eskimos are one race of people, but to disregard variety of custom, tradition, economy and culture is to invite misconception, historic inaccuracy, and stereotype. The native language has a strong continuity throughout Canada and Alaska, but the people, in their different environments, were diverse in dialect, food, clothing, shelter, and custom.

Modern ethnological researches are apt to be a repetition of observations made about only one general area, by the forerunners of today's scientific workers.

Western man has seriously overlooked the chance to use better forms of blending one type of culture with another, utilizing the best of each. Instead, the same destructive methods of the early European "pioneers" are in use today as then. As European man moved west across the United States, the American Indians were pushed aside and dealt with unjustly and brutally whenever it was expedient for the "founding fathers" and their political state. The outcome was the development of a massive bureaucracy stumbling through clumsy and ineffective maneuvers to correct conditions resulting from clear violations of what the founding fathers said was their sacred creed: the Rights and Freedoms of Man. Such "rights and freedoms" are obviously reserved for foreigners only. The Natives were and are still set apart from these privileges of Western man's democracy.

3

Kingetkin: the Village of Wales

In the setting sun, a man is sharply outlined from his immediate surroundings. Quietly occupied with his tasks of ending the day's work, he is self-assured in his movements, as if he had gone through the same pattern repeatedly. Indeed he has, for he is a hunter returned from the hunt in the late evening at Wales, Alaska. The rays of the sun are rapidly elongating, forming colors that strike the surfaces of the snow-covered hills, valleys, houses, and the immediate surroundings. The undisturbed snow crystals around him become millions of reflectors. The deep reds, oranges and yellows of the sun's rays dance between the cool colors of the skies overhead. Shadows form long spears of blue, gray, and blue-green complements to the exposed sides of everything assailed by the setting sun. The nearby hills, which form a crescent-shaped background for Wales, capture most of the light. As in a cinema-scopic screen, reflecting a series of light from some faraway projector, the distant clouds act as multicolored filters, the hills brazenly show themselves off as if to make a spectacular finale of the day's end.

The man is dressed in his hunting apparel, which is equivalent to the every-day wear of any other society, since he is hunting nearly every day. The dogs, dog sled, and the hunting gear are put back in their assigned places for the night. There is a hint of burning spruce and driftwood in the gentle breeze, from the fires in homes: Scattered barking, children's voices, and the thuds of wood-chopping are the only sounds heard. In the Alaskan evening, sounds like these carry for incredible distances. Working hours for this hunting community are long and tedious. During the winter months, daylight hours are short, so the men wake in the dark and prepare for the hunt in the pre-dawn hours. The women have their share of chores also; their main occupations are those of rearing their children and general household caretaking.

This description could be that of a Wales village during the time of Christopher Columbus' famous voyage; or that of more recent times, when my father first began to utilize his knowledge of hunting as a way to make a living. He learned the Eskimo hunting technology, not in the usual ancient way — through his father—but through the sheer necessity of survival. The following pages will, therefore, be an attempt to describe how a young man of Wales endured the intrusion of the white culture, while never quite relinquishing the lessons he had learned in his own Native culture.

Wales is known by its Eskimo name, *Kingetkin,* to those who are most familiar with Northwest Alaska. This spelling by no means is an accurate rendering of pronunciation. The Eskimo language is not taught in the schools of Alaska, even though the majority of those attending schools are Eskimo children. *Kingetkin* means, roughly, "an elevated area", which aptly and simply describes the rocky foothills rising from Cape Prince of Wales due south of the village, enveloping its eastern and northern extremities. The Cape meets the Bering Strait like a mammoth whale sliding into the waters, where the restless sea washes clean the boulders at its mouth. The huge rocks above the water line, black with harsh ebony-hued lichen, darken the Cape. Although it has the bizarre appearance of a threatening monster, the Cape protects the village from the south winds. The other end of the high hill similarly terminates at the northern lowlands above Wales. This northern terminus also bears a resemblance to the head of a whale, if one ignores the massive black rocks jutting out on its ridge like a dinosaur's back. An ancient Eskimo tale has it that an old witch tempted some unsuspecting villagers. They were made to follow her to the mountains, crawling in procession, and then they were turned into stone as punishment. So the rocks were

Hunter using ice testing staff. The hard bone tip is used to probe questionable snow-covered cracks and holes when hunting on ice.

a daily reminder of an ancient legend for the youngsters, a familiar land-mark, and a protector of our ancestral burial site. This ancient burial site is no longer used, because present day missionaries require an underground burial, even in winter time, when snow and ice make it a difficult undertaking. In the summer, there is still the permafrost to contend with. This condition is aptly named. Permafrost occurs as a frozen layer beneath the surface of the top-soil. Thus, in the summer when some of the ice melts, water cannot drain off, and much of the land is covered with swamps and marshes. Farming is not possible in such an area. To dig for burial or any other purpose in such ground, is a task requiring the most arduous physical labor, and extremely impractical.

At the foothills of the Wales mountains, the substance of these rocky heights mingles with the rich soil of the lowlands. Varied vegetation grows, amid lichen-covered rocks and streamlets. During the summer, thousands of birds congregate and nest upon this natural resort for migratory fowl, some hailing from as far away as South America. They provide life, song, and joy for the Wales youth who eagerly set out to explore the wonders of nature, and begin their lessons in Eskimo living, which combine hunting skills with respect for wildlife's wariness of man.

Beneath the foothills, for two miles or so, there stretches a very low, marshy area. Here the streamlets of the hills begin to meet, forming larger streams that flow into deep and narrow canals. Two very prominent mounds break the monotony of the grassy, wet, brownish-red soil between the village and the hills. Each of these mounds is about the size of a football field. They contain the remnants of ancient Eskimo civilizations. Several layers of the same reddish earth are piled up here. Between the layers are frequently found bones, skeletons, stone and ivory utensils, rotted bits of wood, hunting implements, small ivory implements colored with subtle browns, greens, blues and blacks. These are the relics of an era long past. Until the last couple of decades, the villagers had been digging up some of the ivory, which they re-carved into bracelets or tourist trinkets, the result being that the mounds now resemble battlegrounds of trenches and foxholes, facing no enemy except the curious. Since then, the villagers have been informed about a certain law prohibiting excavation of archaeologically interesting sites. And so the mounds rest in peace. The Natives are law-abiding. In fact, there has been only one murder in Wales during the past hundred years. The victim is variously described as an unpopular missionary, or a Bureau of Indian Affairs agent, shot with one of the newly-introduced guns. The gun might very well have been a whaler's gun with an explosive shell.

The village proper is situated on a long wide stretch of gravelly plateau between the lowlands and the beach. The beach is an exceptionally wide expanse of uniform grayish brown sand, abruptly ending on the sea side of the plateau, where the long grass fights a losing battle against the winds, ever shifting the sands and exposing the stringy roots of the brave and hardy tundra grass. In certain areas above Wales, where the beaches are not as wide, the grass actually grows right on the edge of the headlands, holding the sandy earth together, as if to form a huge breaking wave.

The Koughazuk River divides the village into two parts. In my boyhood days, it was connected by a wooden bridge, just wide enough for two people to walk across side by side. The river disappears behind a peak, now called "Old Lady of the Mountains", but not before it narrows at the lowlands to its very deep sections. At some points, it is possible to jump across the river in one long leap, due to the river having etched itself underneath the annually freezing and alternately melting topsoil. Just behind the village, the river widens to a considerable extent, running northward before heading towards the sea through a narrow gap at the bridge site. It never really freezes solid, possibly because it is fed by underground passages from a distant lake. The amount of flowing water seems incredibly voluminous, providing delightfully clear water and solid clean ice sheets. This phenomenon results from the uneven pressures of the running water rushing seaward, and the tidal activity which causes upward leakage from the previous ice formation. One has a choice of either water or ice for home use.

I remember that one of the chores for the village children was to hitch two or three dogs to a small sled and fetch drinking water in large pails which were filled approximately three-quarters full, then topped with chunks of ice to keep the water from spilling during the two mile trip from the starting point of the sandwiched water and ice. The water hole was kept open by means of communal use of the same spot. If the top layer of water "ran dry," an ice chisel was used to open the next layer. Sometimes steps were cut into the uppermost layers of ice and snow, in order to reach the running water beneath. All the homes had storage additions to the living quarters, to accommodate the stored food and water. At times, considerable space was usurped by the piled chunks of ice, which were later melted for bathing and washing clothing.

The wide, frozen surface of the river, just behind Wales Village, offered an unusual if not a dangerous play area for the children. The water sometimes erupts from the top ice layer, to form ultra-smooth bulges, where smooth-bottomed mukluks (Eskimo boots) dared the wearer to stay upright while sliding on them. Other times, the top layer was so newly formed that daredevil kids, running across the strangely undulating, crackling ice, had to face angry parents for unnecessarily wetting their pants and mukluks. Beyond the beach, the Bering Strait extends out to the horizon, where three islands are faintly visible. On clear days, and if one is looking from the hills, the eastern tip of Siberia's Chukchi Peninsula can be seen behind the two larger islands, Little Diomede and Big Diomede. The nearest island, about twenty miles out, is Fairway Rock.

This tiny island becomes a haven for the murre ducks during springtime, when almost every available horizontal surface on it is used for the fish duck's nest. If some of the murres miss their "space reservations" on Fairway Rock, they then nest on the southern side of Cape Prince of Wales, on the rocky bluffs of Tin City, and further down on York and Lost River. The murre ducks lay their eggs on these precarious nesting grounds, consisting of small shelves of solid rock. They are surprisingly large coming from these relatively small ducks, about as large as turkey eggs, and are shaped like a top. The natural tendencies of ordinary eggs would be to roll over the rocky edges, then down either to more rock or to the sea. But shaped as they are, the murre eggs usually do not roll; if this happens, they don't roll very far.

In the winter, the Bering Strait is frozen over for about twenty miles from the mainland coast to the seemingly empty expanse of the sea. Between the ice, the waters, insulated by the snow and ice above, hold much of the food upon which the animals and fish live, and upon which the Wales villagers depend for their own food. Much of the Alaskan coastal areas in the northwest have offshore waters which are shallow trenches at these points, deepening and dropping off at the remainder of the Continental Shelf. Consequently, there is a protective barrier of shallow water, usually about two to five miles out from the shore. In between, there is a deeper but still shallow basin, usually fifteen to twenty fathoms in depth. Many types of fish are found in this shallow place, as well as various types of seals; the common seal with its mediocre fur markings is the most plentiful. Others, less numerous and valued more for their furs than for availability, are the spotted seals, ribbon seals, and the young bearded seals. Further out, usually beyond the shallow ridge, are the larger and less accessible mammals: the adult bearded seal, and the walrus. Very rarely seen are the polar bear, the whale, shark and narwhale.

In fact, the shark is an object of ancient belief which permits its safe passage anywhere it is seen. The Eskimo people believe that a killed shark will bring ill luck to the unfortunate hunter who commits the deed. He will not be successful in catching any more game.

The homeland of my people, the Eskimo, extends from Siberia to Alaska, and on to Canada in her upper reaches, to the Hudson Bay area, then to Baffin Island, ending on the eastern shores of Greenland. The Alaskan coast is similar to coasts found in Norway, Sweden, Canada and other lands north of the tree-line. The Tree-line itself is not a true "line" running a certain distance from the North Pole, which is approximately 1,350 miles north of the northernmost parts of Alaska. This designation is used to describe that area of the north above which trees will not grow. It is more commonly called "timber line." The coasts where I grew up are hilly, and therefore cannot be entirely marshy areas. Almost any given area, from the tundras to the foothills, is a haven for many living organisms: grasses, and more than 700 kinds of flowering plants, mosses, lichens. "Tundra" is a Russian word meaning a "marshy place." Some of the Alaska coast well deserves this descriptive word. However, it really describes only a small part of the Alaskan coast, since a "marshy" place is any level area where it is possible for water to collect.

In the summer, the creeks, running with crystal clear water, are lined on the banks with three or four varieties of willows, often more than ten feet tall. The spring season brings so many different types of birds, fish, and animals, that it would be impossible to deal with each of them here. Wren-sized birds, snipes, curlews, terns, jaegers, sea gulls, ducks, geese, and eagles are only a few of the marvelous species that show themselves during the spring of the year. Field mice, shrews, lemmings, squirrels, rabbits, foxes, wolves, reindeer and bear, join the big parade. Winter birds include the owl and the ptarmigan, the raven and gull. In the waters are fish of all sizes, from needle fish and minnows to trout, arctic char and salmon, flounder, crab, cod, grayling. After stormy weather, the beaches hold clams, mussels and jelly fish. Beyond the shoreline out to sea are the seal and larger mammals.

In the cities, people are raising their voices (a bit late) against the adding of skyscrapers to the skyline, lest the sun and the views of nature's wonders be obscured. In the tundra areas, there is no such problem, but ignorance still defines this beautiful country as "barren." To be able to see the spacious horizon in all directions is something that I well remember, and with nostalgia. Far from being barren, the tundra is alive with organisms and animals of all types and varieties. Everywhere there is life, throbbing with excitement, color, rhythm, and beauty.

Around the Wales area, springtime begins to raid the snows about the middle of April. Although parts of the month of March are sometimes a blinding white, due to the balmy but infrequent sunny days, from April on the days become noticeably longer. Then, the children and other members of the family enjoy being outdoors. Some days are especially warm. May is the month when the migratory birds begin their full-strength invasion of their nesting areas. Phalaropes and snipes choose the melting lakes; the smaller birds have a liking for the grassy beach dunes; and birds of all sizes take to the bases of the hills. Houses lose their snow from the eaves, enough so that tubs of snow water can be collected during the day. Everything seems to burble and wake, even if the night freezes icicles from the melting snow. No matter. The next morning is sure to bring more and more sunshine to erase the snowdrifts on the hillsides, as if a time sequence movie was changing the dead grass and earth from white to browns, reds, grays and yellows. On a clear day in June, the last vestiges of the snow patches fairly steam from the melt. Then the smells of the warm earth rise to mingle with the songs of the birds. The minnows in the pools flit about, leaving a trail of delicate dust in the shallows, like miniature jet trails.

After the fantastic melt, the long summer days turn the warm colors of winter-dead vegetation to the cool colors of summer-greens. Flowers are profuse in yellow, white, orange, purple, blue. The children see nature in its act of replenishment. The bird nests of twigs, grasses, and down (sometimes so well camouflaged that one cannot see them until almost stepped upon), hold eggs of indefinite sizes, shapes and colors. The eggs hatch, and the chicks run about the greens until they suddenly begin to fly, hardly to be distinguished from their parents except for their size.

April and June are also periods when the ice of the Bering Sea begins its transition from solid shore ice, to floating, melting bergs. By the middle of June there is hardly a sign of the vast quantities of shore ice seen during the winters. At first the waters are serene and calm, protected by the remains of the floating, moving ice. July then comes, and the ice finally moves out by action of the tides and currents, so that the sea is either a glimmering shimmer of wavelets, or a gray, roaring mass specked with whitecaps, depending upon the weather.

When the ice is gone and the seal hunting is ended, the men turn their thoughts to fishing, or transporting their families to berry-picking areas. The berries are found in elevations higher than the marshes, and slightly lower than the hilltops. Salmonberries, blueberries, blackberries, cranberries, are picked and placed in sealskin shoulder bags, tin buckets, and wooden kegs. Miles are walked by a family in a single day, searching out the best picking areas. The children, happily tired at the end of the day, rest in camping tents and relish the fresh air, their mouths lined with the stain of the berries.

This, then, is the briefest possible view of my Eskimo land. It has been described as "cruel, stark, undeveloped wasteland, barren." Certainly it gives no special favors to the creatures that pass over it, or live within it. All are welcome to enjoy its bounty, to partake of its many gifts, to live and flourish in its beauty. As for the people who inhabited this land, its discoverers and settlers, my Eskimo ancestors, they came here for a livelihood and not for speculation and exploitation of its resources, nor for personal glory and profit. I think of Columbus, who is credited with "discovery of the New World," as a man who was no doubt a good speculator, planner, and fund raiser, as were the other men who received financial backing from the moneyed people of Europe in those years. All of them are mere inept Johnny-come-latelies in comparison with the First Americans, as they moved from one point of the earth to another. Accepted history books write about the voyages of men such as Columbus as "exciting adventurers." For unadulterated, raw excitement, however, telling the story of man in his noblest endeavors, visualize in your mind's eye these ancestors of mine who moved into a new land. They could not know what lay behind the next hill, or on the other side of the next river. They were always in danger of being trapped by inclement weather, becoming the hunted instead of the hunter. They were explorers of unknown lands, men and women of tremendous courage and fortitude. Surely the First Americans did not all make it safely to the New World — "new" to them, at least twenty thousands of years ago.

These Eskimo peoples have a unique and fascinating history, with cultures entirely different from those of the many Indian tribes, and the Aleuts. To me, the Eskimo of the Alaska-land where I was born, have a rich and exciting heritage. Little of this is known even by Native Alaskans today. Worst of all to endure is the massive quantity of falsification which has accumulated concerning Eskimo history and culture. Such words as "Eskimo, igloo, North Pole, tundra, dog sled, walrus, blubber, mukluk," are made to be synonymous with "harsh, cold, ice, savage, barren, primitive, simple." Thus, a stereotype has emerged of a people without technology, without a culture, lacking intelligence, living in igloos, and at best, a sort of simplistic "nature boy" type of subhuman arctic being.

The beauty of the land is entirely overlooked, as is the intelligence, resourcefulness, and courage of the people.

4

Land and Language

The Innupiat occupy a vast portion of the earth. A look at the map on page 31 shows the Native area. There are certain other important and interesting facts about the people. For example, they are the only Native people living even today in both the Old and the New worlds. From Siberia as part of the Old world, to the North American continent and Greenland, the only separation is in the form of the International Date Line, and the international political borders. Distribution of the Eskimo people ranges from the area of the Bering Strait to the Atlantic coast of Labrador and Greenland, a direct distance of 6,200 miles.

The coastal area is even greater. Alaska itself boasts a coastline of 6,640 miles, a good part of it occupied by the Eskimos. With some few exceptions, notably Eskimos encountered further inland, such as those people near major rivers — the Colville, Kobuk, Noatak, Kuskokwim and Yukon — most make their living on the coast. On the western side of Hudson Bay, the Eskimo area extends inland from the coast some 300 miles. With the exception of Siberia, Greenland, and the Arctic Archipelago north of Canada, the further inland areas are occupied by Indians.

That such a people, occupying this broad expanse of country, with all their variety of dialect, economy, and life style, are still one people, is a fascinating subject in itself. Depending upon environmental and historic conditions, there are considerable similarities as well as differences. In the coastal areas, the large sea mammals such as the whale, walrus, and seal, offer much the same materials for food, clothing, and hunting equipment. On the other hand, the inland Eskimos have a mode of life characteristic of northern inland peoples. The Caribou Eskimo west of Hudson Bay, and smaller groups on the North Slope of Alaska, as well as others in the Yukon-Kuskokwim delta are such "Inlanders."

Eskimo culture before contact with the white man had this advantage for the Native: the ability to be very certain of his ties with his environment and his kind. I say "advantage," because for the modern Eskimo, his ties with his environment and his kind are intermixed with certain critical exterior problems such as dealing with the United States government and its policies, with incoming oil companies as well as with other industries, and all sorts of governmental agencies. These incoming, monied interests require land — and title — to the resources of the country, which makes it difficult for the original inhabitants to realize that this land is a transferrable entity which can change hands through certain paper work and an exchange of money. To the pre-white-contact Eskimo, the land was for all of its inhabitants, whether they be Eskimo, foxes, bears, birds, vegetation, or a combination of all these, plus the earth, air and water. This type of understanding of the land and its uses is still common for many Alaska Eskimos.

I was born a Coastal Eskimo. Naturally, any deviation from this culture was a significant change for me and my people. We could communicate with the Caribou Eskimos, and the other Inlanders, except for those from south of the Yukon. We could understand their dialects. However, since they do not hunt seal, walrus, and other sea mammals, they were "Nunnamuit," or translated roughly into English, "From the Inland." In turn, they thought of us as "Immikmuit," or "From the Waters." Earlier weapons of the Nunnamuit and the Immikmuit were the bow and arrow for the Inlanders, the harpoon or spear for the coastal Eskimos. These major differences in hunting tools are generally what differentiate the Innupiats as to their local cultures. But, they all know themselves as "Innupiat."

One recent television feature about the Eskimos explained that Eskimos speak of snow in more than a dozen words, and yet do not have words for time itself, nor of the passage of time.

Where was it that I learned "Sussak" means approximately *an hour?* That *"Oogeyak"* means the *time of fall?* "Uflahmi" means *last year.* "Nahnahkun" is the word for *after a while.* "Oovlakun," designates *tomorrow.* The word "Oobluk" translates to *the moon.* There are many other Eskimo words defying such a brazen falsification of Eskimo culture and language. We have special words to designate springtime, summer, the sun, the stars, day.

Other Eskimo words, interesting because they show the culture of the Eskimo as reflected in their language, are these:

The word "Twakh" means *person,* the plural being "Twadt," *persons.* For "Man" our word is *Ahngnooteh.* "Woman" is *Ahngnuk.* Plurals for these two words, respectively, are *Ahngnoodit,* and *Ahgnut.* The word for "Boy" is *Illigaruk*; that for "Girl" is *Niaksak.* Our designation of the word "Tot," or "Little One," is *Mukshurahk.* And so on, each with its own and varied plural. These words can mean *any* people, *any* man, *any* persons: Innuit, Inuk, Twakh, Tdwadt. The term *Innupiak*, which translates to "Real man," is the only word that can be said to mean "Eskimo." In our family, even so, the actual translation is lost and now means "Ordinary Eskimo," with no emphasis on the "Real" in mind.

I have very often heard my father say, "Innu piah poh rut!" I can only translate this to: "Men who are real and those who are poor, little, despicable." These are the words he uses when he has heard of some Eskimo, or Eskimos, who act as bad examples to young people for instance. To him, no literal translation is implied; what he is saying is, "Those pitiful people — who happen to be Eskimos." It would also have an entirely different meaning, depending upon whether he was smiling or not. If he smiled, it might be an expression of admiration for a notable example. If there was elongation of the syllables, and stress at the end of the phrase, it would have quite the opposite meaning. Since Eskimo is not a written language, this simplification of the number of words, used to describe so much, becomes a very complex thing, as compared to another, written, language.

This foretaste of a language other than English, a Native language which is a thousand-years' predecessor of the "foreign" English spoken now, is for the purpose of suggesting a different culture, a different value-system, entirely different sounds, lifeways, experiences. In my opinion, Americans are the most provincial people in the world. Where we Eskimos and other Native peoples respect another language and other cultures, the people who brought a European culture to our lands display the utmost disrespect for the speech of others, which sound "strange" to them. One might ask: What is it to be "strange?" Certainly it is associated with the sounds of unfamiliar languages, and ignorance of different ways of life. But one need not display arrogance and disrespect. For example: the words Wop, Sheeny, Gook, Digger, Chink, or Jap, are used by many Americans to describe peoples with languages other than English, cultures other than "American," if there can be said to be an American culture. These are slanderous terms.

In the same way, foreigners who came to the land of the Innupiat corrupted Eskimo or Indian words, rendering them unrecognizable from the original Native word. Or, new words were introduced, which the Natives adopted into their own language, since usage became universal by those who sought to trade with us. The words *Mukluk* and *Igloo* are cases in point. The Eskimo words for these are, respectively, *Kuhmik,* and *Inni.* Today, many original Native words are lost because of trade usage of the new vocabulary. Nevertheless, the Eskimo language and its dialects remain relatively intact, although many borrowings are included today. Perhaps, one of these times, this beautiful ancient tongue will be considered important enough for survival, even with the additional borrowings. Why not teach the Eskimo language in the schools of Alaska, where the Native peoples constitute the majority of the population, or at least a great part of the population. When I went to school, we were not allowed to speak our own language. Much of it was lost in this way.

Among the Northwestern Alaskan villages, the varying dialects are practically the only differences recognized by each village as tribal differences, if they can be said to exist. Even so, these are considerable differences. An interesting facet of life is that each small village, usually set apart by a hundred miles or so from another, tends to nurture what can best be described as country gossip. This "gossip" is part pastime, and part weapon. It does not, however, alienate the villages except in extremely rare cases. The reason for this is that gossip is generally spread by the men who travel from village to village. Usually they have a large amount of understanding of human nature. The "gossip" they spread is generally informative, or they would not be made welcome in any village, their own or any other. I remember, in my own Wales village life, that these travelers were very much like goodwill ambassadors. They seemed to spread so much laughter and joy — both to themselves, and to the host family. This was true especially at meal times, when the whole family would squat down on the floor, enjoying all those good foods which the host usually saved for such occasions. In my life, I have been a little sorry not to have had the opportunity of becoming a traveling Eskimo hunter-fisherman.

I always thought it would be such great fun to be a traveling guest in an Eskimo village. Even in recent times, my father and a good part of our family have made skinboat trips to Teller and Wales, from Nome where he now lives. On their return, they have always had the most gleeful things to say about each village. And each family that was especially kind to us was not forgotten if they ever ventured to Nome; my father would try to help them as much as possible, with equal kindness. This is the old-time Eskimo, or Innupiat way.

To conclude this brief foray into the green fields of cultural differences, the word *Eskimo* itself is not one belonging to the Innupiat. It was used, but with a different sound, by the Indian Abnakis and certain other tribes. In *their* language, it means "eaters of raw meat."

SIBERIA
Arctic Ocean
Asiatic Eskimos
Bering Strait
N. Alaskan Coast Eskimos
North Alaskan Inland Eskimos
Bering Sea Eskimos
ALASKA
Athabascan Indians
Pacific Eskimos
Mackenzie Eskimos
Copper Eskimos
Netsilik Eskimos
Caribou Eskimos
Igloolik Eskimos
Baffinland Eskimos
Polar Eskimos
Baffin Bay
GREENLAND
West Greenlanders
East Greenlanders
ICELAND
Arctic Circle
Davis Strait
Atlantic Ocean
Hudson Strait
Hudson Bay
Labrador Eskimos
Northwest Coast Indians
CANADA
Algonkian Indians
Salisch Indians
Sioux Indians
"LOWER FORTY EIGHT"
Pacific Ocean
Lands Occupied by Eskimos
Present Day
Evidence of Prehistoric Sites Occupied by Eskimos

Flounder Fishing Through Ice In Winter

In the cold, clear winter days at Wales, the flounder fisherman plans for at least a half-day out on the shore ice. The fishing hole is chiseled with the "touk" and the bone and baleen fishing hole ice-scoop is used to keep the water clear for better visibility.

The long, slender spear with ivory barbs is held with the right hand. The lure does not have a hook. It is cleverly made of ivory and shaped like a small flounder. It is manipulated with the left hand, causing it to wriggle and flit about to simulate the fish.

The flounder fishing windbreak is fashioned from the jagged chunks of ice residue made by the pressure ridges of the shore ice.

A cutaway view is shown herewith.

The Skinboat Hunting Crew

Before white contact, the skinboat was an important big game hunting transportation method for the Eskimos. During those early centuries, magnificent hunting fleets were customary, rather than today's occasional, one crew, mechanized expeditions. The sail and the paddles were silent propellants of these crafts, filled with men who made a good living from the sea, and led a satisfying life because of it.

Today one hears the crack of the rifle and the unceasing throb of the outboard motors, spoiling the air and ruining the hunt.

There is still the skinboat; the parka still exists as well as other durable Eskimo clothing. The paddles, harpoon and the skinboat construction itself join with the memories which move today's Eskimo hunters in Northwest Alaska to continue this age-old tradition.

Interior of the Khazghi

Modern day Eskimo hunting sled

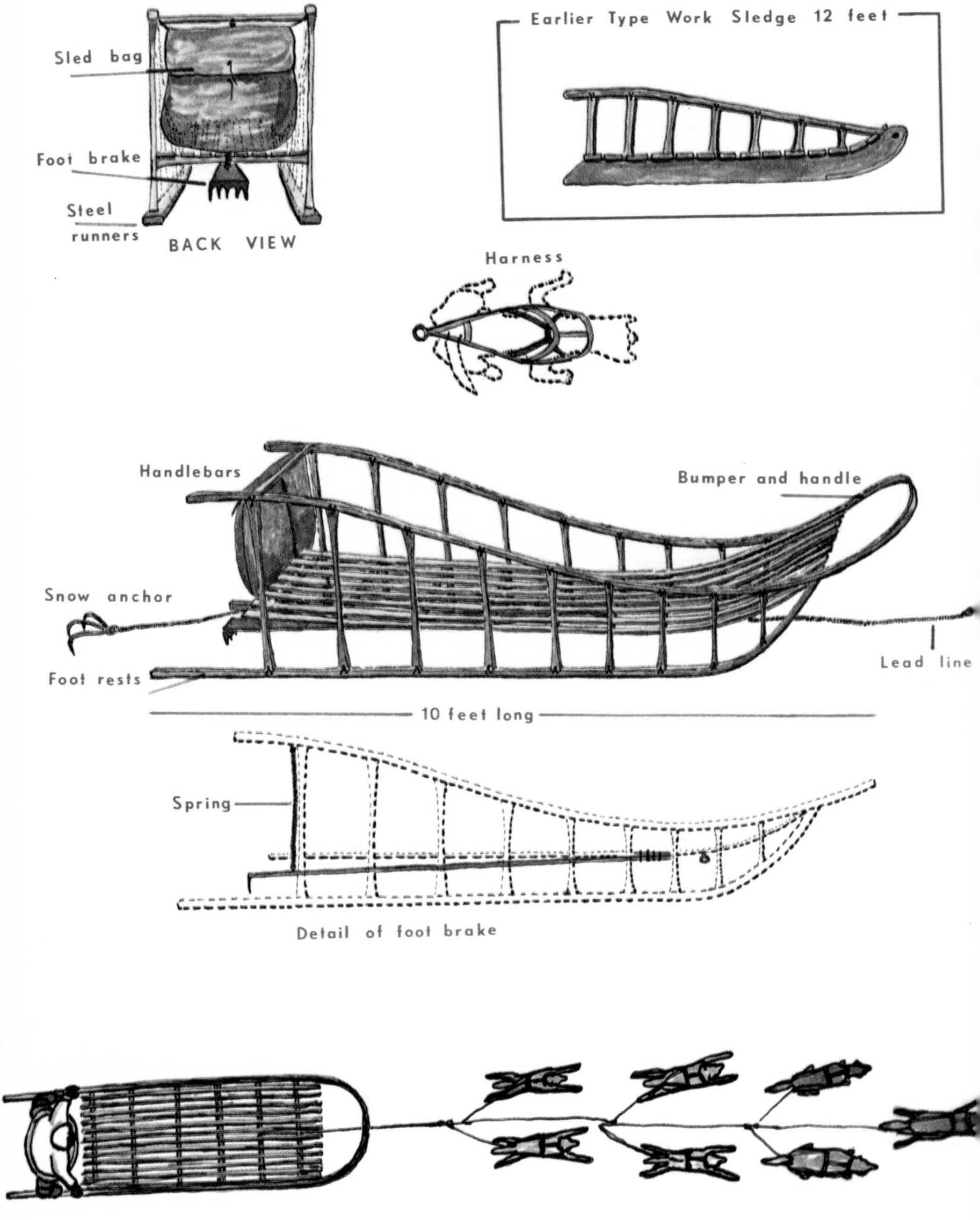

Sled bag

Foot brake

Steel runners

BACK VIEW

Earlier Type Work Sledge 12 feet

Harness

Handlebars

Bumper and handle

Snow anchor

Lead line

Foot rests

10 feet long

Spring

Detail of foot brake

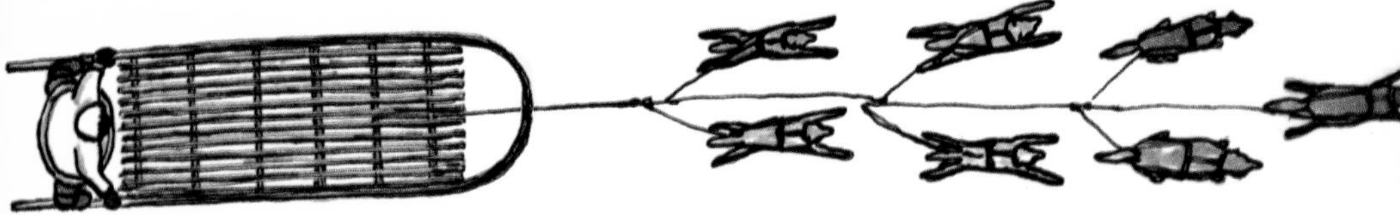

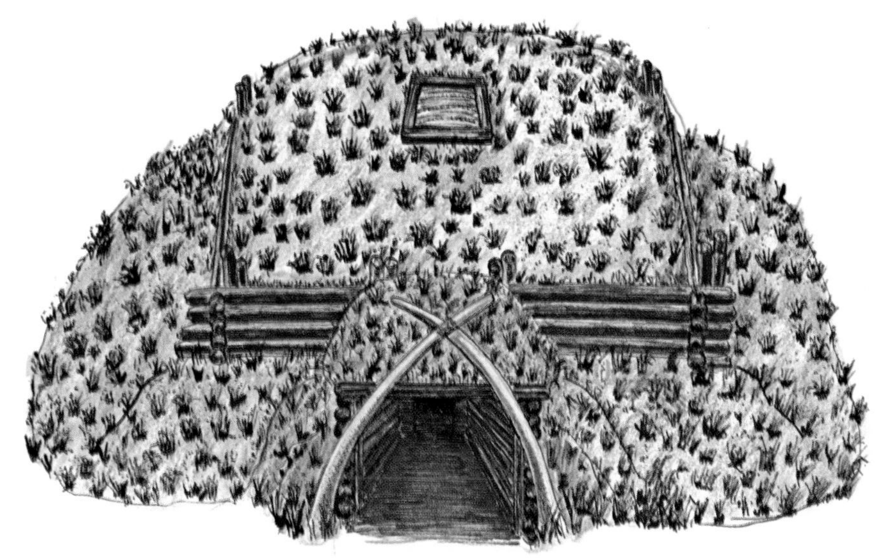

Two Views of the Exterior of a Khazghi

Eskimo Ceremonial House of the
Wales Area in
Northwestern Alaska

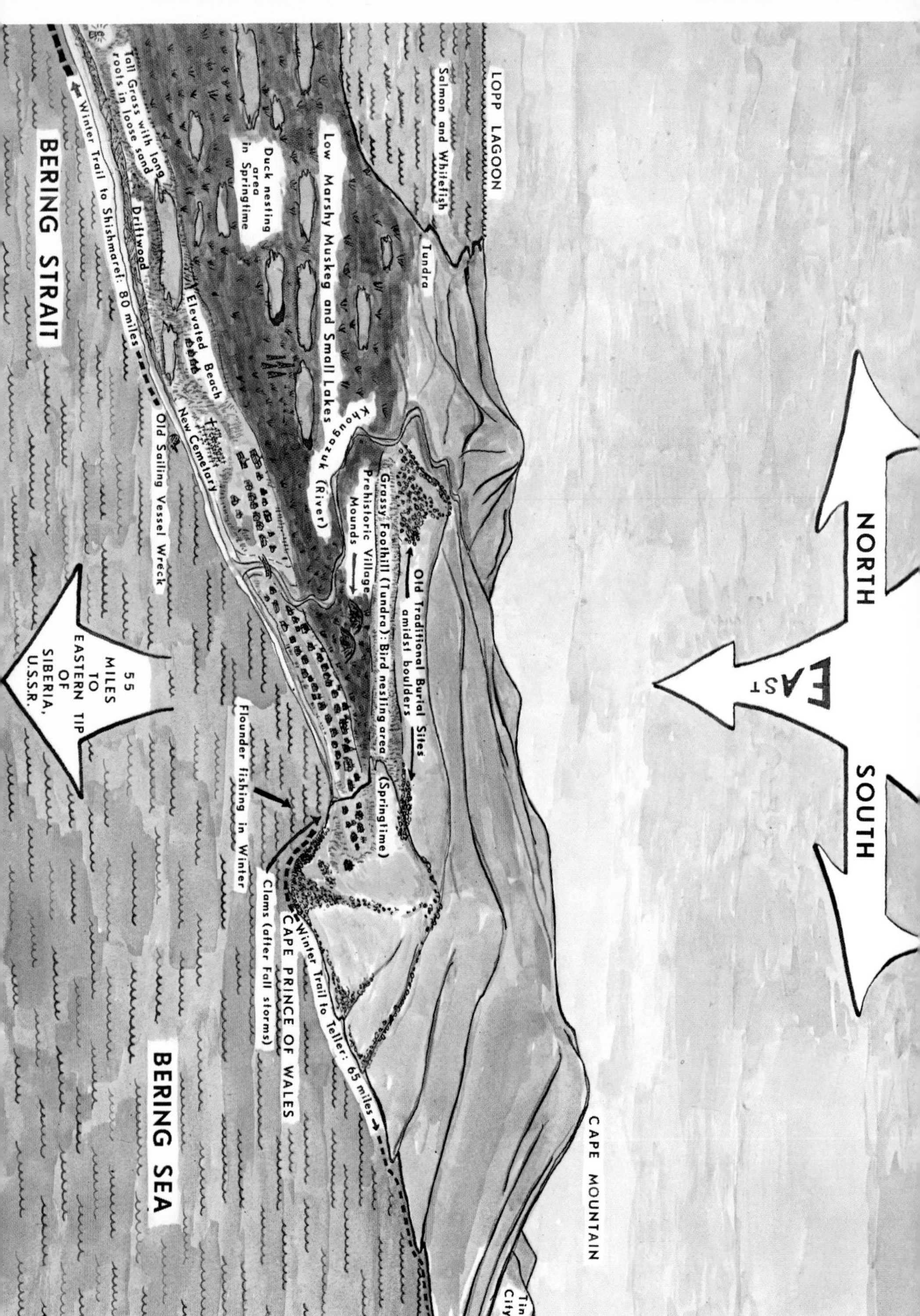

Wales Village Environment. The Village is Northwest of Cape Prince of Wales

5

Village and Family

Each Spring, the village of Wales rediscovers the joy of having survived another winter, a specific cycle of a whole world contained within the few square miles of the village. All human needs were provided for, one way or another. True, some men moved out to join other villages, or other villagers moved to Wales. But this did not add to the social life. Neither did it diminish our lives.

One of the ways the villagers welcomed springtime was to gather up all the "Ik tah zhuck," or discards. Everyone contributed to the Ik tah zhuck, and piled them on sleds: Things used during the winter which could not then be discarded, since everything was used in the dead of winter; socks with holes, worn gloves and mittens, shredded underwear, reindeer hide bedding with the fur dropping off in clumps. Added to these items were old woolen blankets so worn as to resemble contemporary weaving with appropriately placed holes, random in size and location, parka covers ripped here and there and no longer white as when new, other articles of clothing which had to make do until the need came for new spring hunting outfits.

All this had the wives busily sewing and repairing fixables, and producing new items. From the food storage areas came waste like cans of rancid seal oil, blubber from the many fat seals caught during the winter, meats that could no longer be kept in the cold storage rooms due to lack of space. The underground "cold storages" were cleaned out and prepared for the new spring catches.

Since the invention of the kerosene lamp and the gasoline lantern, introduced at a later time to the village, the extra seal oil and blubber was not used. To throw it away during the winter would be almost sacrilege, until definite prospects existed of obtaining more in the spring. Sometimes it took two or three sled loads per family to empty the houses of unwanted winter savings. The sled was hauled by the young people. This was because, if the dogs were used for pulling the sleds, they would become too sprightly and endanger spilling waste matter on the clean trailways leading to the open waters. The stuff was not brought all the way to the edge of the shore ice. It was deposited about two miles out, so that the spring melting would break the ice away, the currents and tides carrying the ice and junk together out to sea. Although it was hard work, the young people found in it a chance to combine work and play on a big scale. For me, young as I was then, it was a chance to learn about the type of ice existing away from the near shore. Huge, impending mounds of pressure ridges offered a chance to climb upon them and look at the open waters two or three miles out, shimmering water dazzlingly brilliant under a bright, warm sun. The land behind the panorama of snow, rocks, yellow-brown grass, and the village, contained a scattering of happy gray house roofs emitting white plumes of smoke, and people looking like midgets walking about, sawing firewood, cleaning up, feeding dogs. Clean air. If a commercial advertisement happens to say anything about "clean as all outdoors," I happen to be fortunate enough to know what it really means.

The sea gulls, ever present scavengers, were around to compete with the ravens. Both types of birds voicing their squawks of "Kaw gleek!" and "Caw Caw!" Soaring and diving and diving and soaring for the pieces of blubber. This occurs just before the other migratory birds have winged their way from the South, and the two obnoxious sounding birds have the whole seashore to themselves. That is, besides the children — ourselves. Even if some play was involved in this chore, we knew it was not proper to stay out any longer than to dump the trash and head back to the village. To play too long on the ice meant getting our clothes wet, or causing parents to worry. This was not a wise thing to do while so far away from the warmth of the stove and the house. Not to mention the scolding one would get for carelessness and stupidity. Besides, it was a rather proud moment, to be aware of having been of some help to the family while still so young. In the late afternoon, the sun was still far enough away during early Spring to allow rapid cooling of the air above the ice as the sun set. The walk home involved being subjected to this cooling. Therefore the eagerness to get off the windy snow and ice.

If the wind got really active, the whole foot or so of blowing snow atop the ice, around the pressure ridges, would begin an eerie snake dance of white. During stronger winds, this layer would lift, to become five feet of blinding, crisp, fast moving snow. This is not precipitation, but actually drifting snow. Even a slight wind creates a certain deft movement of curious patterns, especially on top of solid ice or hard packed snow. This loose snow, of earlier snowfall at another place, has truly walked the surface of the earth, and sometimes even the open water leads. Who knows where it has fallen originally? Or when?

Back at the house, the cleanup is nearly finished except for one daily chore, so necessary in a village without flush-type toilets, or even a sanitary system such as Nome has, which is a truck that makes calls at the homes to pick up the "honey buckets." Even in conditions such as the winds and blowing snow in the winter and blowing sands in summer, the "slopbuck" (Eskimo corruption for "slopbucket") had to be hand carried to the seashore. In the spring, the mounds of frozen darkness broke off with the rest of the shore ice, and were carried away to melt, and finally to sink many miles away. These mounds of human excrement often resembled dark animal forms to the hunter. Unless his eyes were keen, many stalked their own waste products before realizing their mistake. Today, "civilization" has so far reached us, that some homes even have outhouses.

In Wales, when people meet, they do not use the salutation so familiar to western man. One did not feel the need of a "How do you do?" Or an informal "Hi!" Or a handshake. Not even a nose-rub. Even the translated "Kanook itpin," for "How are you," is merely a literal translation from the English, as are many other

Eskimo phrases for Native greetings now. Small talk was made whenever the impulse for such talk overcame a person, and when he felt that the listener had the time to rest a bit from whatever he was doing in order to listen.

If a person wanted to visit someone, rather to visit some *family,* since there was no real need to build strong defensive ties with individuals, all he had to do was to walk into the family home. As a child, if my brothers and sisters had gone out to work or play with their peers, and I was left to myself, I would either go to any interesting area of activity, where maybe only mature persons normally went. I would watch silently. Or, I would walk into a home where I knew children of my age were living. For instance, I might walk into one house and find the older persons at home working or preparing dinner, and the young not at home. One of the elders might look up from his or her work and say one word, "Pee-lut." This means, "They are not here." I now have the option either to watch the work process, or leave quietly to go on to another home. Doors were never locked, and no one I can remember has ever been told to get out of a private house because of being unwelcome.

There was, however, a recognized rule that a family — and especially the children — did not roam around to different houses in the evening after supper. This left the individual families with a certain assured time for privacy. Unless there was some special occasion arranged for groups of families, such as celebrations of successful hunting expeditions with huge communal meals, this was the understood rule, respected and observed by all.

My parents were dead set against their children knowing very much about sex. "Nature will take its own course," was the general philosophy. In fact, most of Wales, young and adult, was of the same temperament. However, some of the Wales children were being exposed to outside influences and it was noticeable that these few youngsters had acquired measurable quantities of sexual knowledge not discussed or realized by the traditional Wales child. Here again, it was not always on the excessive side (if one can define what "excessive" in this case means). As an example, one of the families went to the Lower-Forty-Eight for a circus type performance and came back to Wales without any recognizable detrimental effects. Their children have grown up in as much a natural manner as can be expected under Wales conditions. It may have been due to the very early age of this family's two children at the time, so that "civilization" did not have a chance to affect them. Sex was a natural thing, part of life, not for play or casual emotional experimentation.

At this time in Wales, the missionaries had succeeded in causing the Eskimo family man to be fearful of mentioning "nasties" — meaning anything about sex, to the young. One day I distinctly overheard a neighbor man refer to his Alaska Territorial Guard rifle as an "A.T.G. . . . " followed by a completely unfamiliar word. I ran home for supper and after the meal I disclosed the strange way in which Toby referred to his rifle, to Mom and the rest of the family. There was a curious silence for a moment, while Dad and Mom pondered the precisely unobtrusive way of bringing the embarrassing situation to a close. Finally, in her rarely used gruff voice, Mom asked me never to say the word again. I stood silent for a while, wondering what was so bad about repeating what a grown man had said. Thereafter, I rarely heard the English word used by anyone, although the Eskimo term was frequently whispered and joked about by my older playmates. The missionaries had no need to harp on this subject either. Villagers very willingly accepted the fact that their children should grow up to be good Christians, whatever that may be.

I really don't remember just what the Presbyterian Church taught as its underlying philosophy, although the villagers always went to church on Sundays and holidays. The village council was probably the main target for the church officials, in order to disclose or discover the evils and bad habits of the Eskimo.

Church day in Wales. No matter what the weather was, Sunday was a time to don the best mukluks, the nicest looking knit gloves, and whatever else added to the scrupulously clean look. After a week of going to school in whatever clothes were available, Sunday meant hunting around for the niceties. Therefore, waking up time was a little earlier, and breakfast was eaten a little faster, so that there would be time to find the Sunday clothes. These were not much different from daily attire in our family. Usually, they were simply cleaner and less worn looking. Except for my adopted sister. She was the little girl of the family, and she would be decked out in clean, light brown cotton stockings, a frilly dress from Sears, and bright colorful parka cover. She started out, as a child, with extraordinarily sparse hair, so what hair she had would be braided as far as possible in two little pigtails at the back of her small head. Then, when everyone was ready, the whole family walked to the church. Over the two or three well-sized snow drifts, along the three-quarters of a mile, we went to church. On the way, we met other families walking, with that extra air of pride in clothes and general appearance.

Each family kept within its own group during the walk to church. A certain sense of selfconsciousness prevailed. Perhaps the lack of lively conversation was due to the fear of being accused of gossiping. The missionaries preached of sin through gossiping, and the church-goers did not wish to have it thought they were indulging in this sinful practice. Even our own family didn't have much to say during the 15 or 20-minute walk. My brother and sister and I would sometimes hold hands, not wanting to act childishly in the eyes of our parents. We were not allowed to tumble and slide on the snowdrift drop-offs, and that too held us under control. It was like going to school, without being able to sneak in a cops and robbers chapter with other children.

During this part of the week, it seemed to me that Mom and Dad really enjoyed the opportunity to do something outdoors as a family. In earlier days, however, a family get-together was not plucked out of one day of the week. The Khazghi, or Eskimo community house, which we passed every Sunday and is now seen as a seldom used artifact, was where handsome and clean clothes were not prerequisites for the meetings. However, a richness of pride in knowing what to do and how to execute the Eskimo dance movements probably brought out the best in everyone who went to the ceremonies at the Khazghi. In those days, and in that way, in that place, *this* was indeed our family day, and God, in my day it was the beginning of an end. The end of age-old customs and the beginning of the worship of western, artificially handsome clothes.

At the church, which was simply a larger version of the typical house in Wales, we would industriously sweep the snow from our mukluks at the storm shed. Two or three big brooms were furnished for this purpose. For the children, such as Cora and me, it was more like wrestling with a vaulting pole.

But we had to show respect for the church of God, and enter without making the floor wet. The outside door kept the elements out, but the inner entrance to this, the biggest room in Wales, was a double door of dark stained oak. Often we would be entering through this door, just as one of the older men, who volunteered his services to the church, was just ending his vigorous pulling of the church bell rope. This bell was one of the marvels of mechanics in my eyes, and when the snows piled up outside almost to the steeple, I liked to stay outdoors a while longer to watch the old gears and ropes moving when they made that noise.

When the services started, the missionary cited from the Bible, as an interpreter translated. The songs were alternately sung in English and then in Eskimo. The collection plate was passed around. More songs. The people then streamed out towards their homes. I really doubt that the collection plate earned much for the Wales church. Our father would give us at most three pennies to put into the plate. At this time, I thought that a nickel was worth quite a bit. Unlike the fervent be-damned or be-saved atmosphere of some churches, it was more like going to a place to be forewarned about things that *might* come to mind in any normal life and yet be considered sinful in the eyes of those whose job it is to save the souls of people. This kind of teaching was absorbed quietly by the Wales villagers. The singing, accompanied by the foot operated organ, played by a self-taught family, was earnest in its efforts. One or two bass singers and a couple of sopranos were leaders of the singing, which tended to be more soprano than anything else. It was always noticeable when the men did not fully express themselves in singing in a low, manly voice or a loud voice. Their singing was always subdued by their desire not to stand out before anyone else, lest one be considered a show-off. This wish for not seeming to emulate anyone or anything showed up repeatedly, and in many ways. One didn't need to advertise anything or anyone in Wales. Everyone to his own place was the custom, and that place was held to be nothing lower or higher than that of anyone else, wherever or whatever it might be.

This general description of modern church-going, which really is somewhat of a social moré today, and little else, contrasts sharply with our own culture, our own social and religious experience as Eskimo people. Observances of a social nature, as well as those of a ritual type, were accompanied by singing and some type of dance. The Eskimo dance is performed with a built-in ebullience. The male voice is in step with the beat of the drum.

The drum is made of carefully chosen driftwood, usually a rare cottonwood or ash. A walrus-stomach lining is stretched over this frame. The wood is shaped, or rather adapted, to the final form, to take the punishment of the two or three types of stresses incurred in stretching the resonant walrus membrane, as well as hitting and hammering of the drumstick. The wood is shaped, however, to only about a quarter-inch thickness and a couple of inches in width. The drumstick is also shaped to conform to the individual shape of the drum and the player's hand. In earlier days, the handle of the drum was made of various substances, from ivory to whalebone, and its shape was carved into ornate and subtle animal forms.

With voices screeching and breaking from the call to perform, to the sounds of the drum, the men would visibly perspire and strain to keep the dance at a frenzied pace, once the opening stanzas were cautiously elaborated upon. Quite a difference from the ritual practically forced upon the Wales folk today!

The emphasis placed on clothes, in connection with church-going, reminds me of the often curious ways in which some Eskimo people respond to city ways, city dress and customs, and western ideas of style. Our own idea of beauty in clothing was utilitarian, and in step with our available supplies of furs, skins, shells, and ivory. Items that were rare and available only from a distance by way of trade with other tribes, were usually considered of greater value. Naturally, since the amount of time and energy expended in getting these things was so much greater. But I well remember that the man of one family, returning from Nome, brought back

THE ESKIMO DRUM

An orchestra of seven or eight experienced Eskimo singers and drummers getting into full swing is an experience hard to forget.

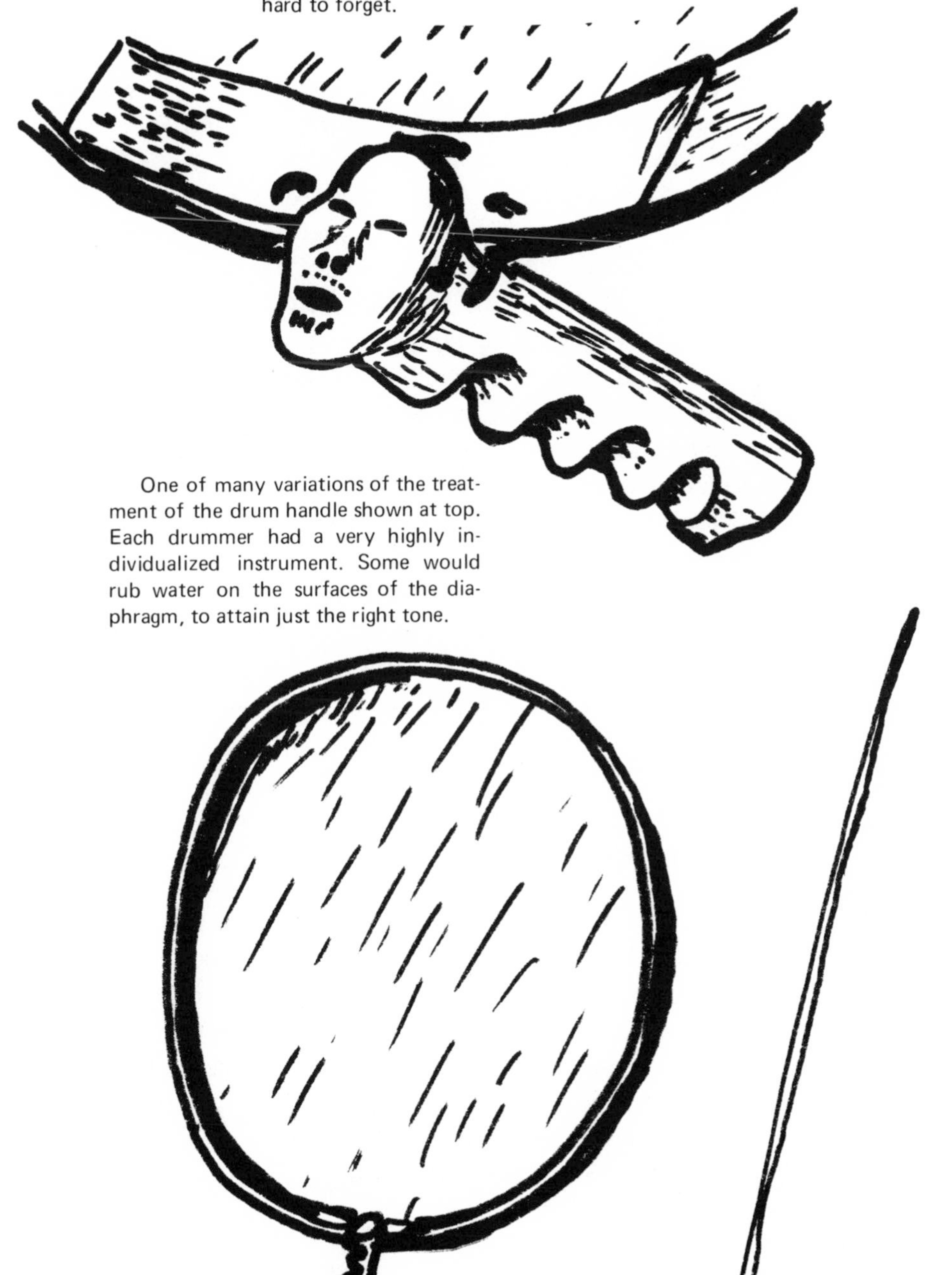

One of many variations of the treatment of the drum handle shown at top. Each drummer had a very highly individualized instrument. Some would rub water on the surfaces of the diaphragm, to attain just the right tone.

with him an irrepressible urge to dress in such regalia as a fedora hat and business suit, during the few Christian holidays observed in Wales. Amidst the parka covers cleaned by means of the old washboard, and the use of either hand-cranked wringers or good strong hands, he strutted in his "soodagloke" (suit of clothes), and always appeared in clean-shaven state. This display of new-found finery attracted the attention of such as my mother, who would prophesy: "Someday, sons, if you work and study hard, you too will be able to wear soodagloke."

Another young man, who subscribed to and assiduously read comic magazines, carved much ivory so that he could order a suit. But he apparently did not make enough for the hat or shoes. He would join the Fourth of July outings dressed in his wrinkled, striped suit, the pants bulging forward at the knees, the cuffs rolled up, and the jacket hem around his mid-thighs. For a hat, he had on his blue baseball type hunting hat, the sun visor jauntily rolled upward in a sweeping curve. His feet were royally encased in rich calfskin mukluks with shiny beads on the top edges, just underneath his rolled-up, untailored slacks.

I was no exception to such results of a foreign style-system. However, it must be said that often such "styles" in clothing were forced upon us because of the lack of native materials, and the easy accessibility of the foreigners' clothing. There was a man in Nome who eked out additional income through purchasing children's used clothing from the church rummage sales, at about 25¢ an item. These were then sent to Wales for re-sale at 50¢ an item. I used to wear some of these clothes. One I remember most was a jacket two or three sizes too small. But it was relatively new looking, smelled freshly clean, and it had a zipper front. It also had a knit collar. The cuffs of this jacket were near my elbows, and the knit waist near my ribs. I wore it for "dressing up" in the summertime. With this garment, I wore a pair of knee-length rubber boots, faded denim overalls, and a light blue cotton shirt. For a cap, I had the leather "flying ace" contraption with plastic goggles. From Sears. Since this was considered so "dressy," by my family in those days, there is still a snapshot kept of me and a playmate, who was not so dressed up. His attire was more that of the conventional Wales Eskimo boy, a parka with a white parka cover. Except for his cap, which was just like mine.

In the winter, all this disappeared into the clothes bags, and I emerged with mukluks, a pair of longjohns, the same faded denim overalls and a parka with a rotted chin area from the frost when playing in the snow. About this time, my brother and I were almost the same height and the same size school clothes was ordered for both of us; from Sears, or occasionally from the village store. Mom sewed the parka covers from very thick cotton twill, with the miniature hunter's bib pocket which she always reminded us not to fill with snow while playing. Somehow, it always ended up wet anyhow. We had a hard time identifying our own gloves, my brother and I. Or, our own pair of pants, or socks. So it became older brother's prerogative to take the better garment, if the argument got too noisy for the rest of the family to endure.

Even today, I think too much care and attention is given to style in dressing the outer man. I like to be comfortable.

6

The Seal Hunt: Nik-Sak, Umiak-Tuk and Khazghi

In our Wales environment, the people were tightly woven together as a community. Each family was interdependent with four or five other families; and all worked as one hunting party. This hunting crew had for its leader the owner of the large skinboat, called an *Umiak.* The Umiak is approximately thirty to thirty-five feet long, about eight feet wide at the widest point, and five feet high at the bow. Each of the four or five-member crew usually brought along the eldest son as a fledgling crewman, thus increasing the total crew to 10 or 12, as the case might be.

In order to take care of a village of 150 inhabitants, the Wales men had at their disposal a minimum of five or six crews which plied the waters for seals, the main staple food. There were, of course, more than five or six boats available. Care was taken to keep the best boats in top condition, however, and to do this the full manpower was needed. Indeed, maximum reliability was required of such a craft during the spring hunting season. In the months of March and April, preparations of the collective village workers at the embarkation sites of the skinboats and at the Khazghi, reflected the imminence of springtime and all its promise to young and old alike. The Khazghi is an ancient communal building, the only authentic village house, in the true Eskimo style, left in Wales. Today, all the houses are, in outward appearance, straight-line, with gabled roof, the sort of frame structure so familiar in the old western frontier towns of America. Thus, the Eskimos of Wales have conceded to the building designs of an alien culture, however inadequate to the local climate. The type of structure advocated by the early missionaries and schoolteachers now generally prevails. Thus have my people bartered away a good way of life for ideological "acceptance."

The survival of the Khazghi and the skinboat deserves some mention at this point. Both are still used by the villagers, but as more and more modernization is stressed by western technology, and as more influence is exerted by the Christianizing missionaries upon younger Eskimos, the people themselves are slowly becoming victims of a defeated and unsatisfying way of life. It is not recognized that the Eskimo types of structures and crafts comprise a perfectly valid and efficient technology, well suited to the land and the needs of the people, even today. Designs of both the Khazghi and the skinboat evolved through centuries of invention and experimentation. Their efficiency and durability have been proven, and neither the new types of homes nor the new types of boats are as efficient, particularly when few if any Eskimos can afford either the one or the other.

The Khazghi was once the church, the townhouse, workshop, and entertainment center, all in one, before the onslaught of missionaries and European-acculturated schoolteachers. After the erection of the new church and schoolhouse, it was considered foolish to tear down the old Khazghi. So it stood as a silent reminder of the days when the Ahnghakook, or medicine man, told his stories, when the men of the village celebrated their catches, and (not too long ago), when the influential leaders of the village met and pondered the question of allowing the intruding white culture into their confidence. The exterior of the Khazghi does not shout out its presence. Rather it is like an extension of the whole countryside. Driftwood was used for its sides; but unlike a log cabin, it is further fortified with sod, almost to the top of the structure. The roof is also made of rough hewn driftwood logs laid against a shaped log which is placed lengthwise along the top of the shallow gable. Then it too is covered with sod, which grows green with grass during the summer. Near the top is an opening with translucent animal tissue, used in the days before the introduction of cold glass.

The interior of the Khazghi is entered only through the south side. This entrance, also made of logs, is unusually long, about twelve feet long by five feet high and four feet wide. The inner doorway is slightly smaller, about three feet wide and four feet high, so that it could be easily protected by a skin door. The interior seems extraordinarily spacious, due to the sunken floor. The floor space measures about eighteen feet square. The west, or door side, is bare earth to the middle north-south division, where it is covered by wide planks to the eastern wall. Along the north, east, and south walls, above the floor planks, are benches attached approximately three feet from the floor, about eighteen inches wide. The height of the wall extends for another four feet from the seats, and the center of the room is about ten feet high.

Even today the Khazghi is used as a place in which to sew the walrus skins together for the skinboats. Walrus hides are prepared by first splitting the skins in thickness, so that there are two sizeable hides instead of one, which is unworkable in its original state. The women spend much of their time in a sort of quilting-bee common work session, utilizing their skills to the fullest extent. During such sessions the activity is of an almost frenzied nature. Everyone is busy.

Some of the older women are "captains" of the group, and are responsible for the final fitting of the skins onto the boat frame by the men. All work together and each knows his or her task. Refitting the skins to the boat frame must be done every one and a half to two seasons, when the salt water has started to soften the quarter-inch or so of hide. I will not pretend that I know the entire technological process of tanning hides, or measuring correct dimensions for the boats, which generally vary in size. I was only a small boy running around with other small children, when witnessing these highly skilled operations, which developed over centuries of living and working in the Wales environment. However, even at the age of six, the actual witnessing of these operations by the skilled people of the older generation was the beginning of the learning process for the average young villager. I was no exception. After splitting the hides, the heavy halves are soaked to soften them for the next technique, which is to patch all the punctures and weak spots resulting from the hunt, or from the skinning or splitting part of the process. After this, the hides are cut to shape, and some of the more experienced sewers are assigned to their specialties in each section of the boat covering.

It takes about a week to see a recognizable shape forming out of the mass of yellowish, cream colored, tanned hides, and about a day's work by the men to stretch the hide over the inverted boat frame. Division of labor in the old times was generally by family. Families of the early Wales village specialized in certain sections of skinboat maintenance: making parts of the boat frame, repair of the part, selection of materials, sewing of the sections. This division of labor made it possible for the specializations to be handed down to children and grandchildren by the parents. As in any group participation of any society, the experienced ones had their opportunity to shine with pride of accomplishment during these preparations for the spring hunt. While I watched, I remember my parents were noticeably eager to be of help in any way they knew. Since they were raised without parents to teach them any specialties, they learned by questioning those who were experienced, by intelligent observation, and by working.

While the Khazghi is now used more for mundane community projects than as a center of Eskimo village society, as it was in the past, it is still a standing monument of my ancestral life. With the missionaries came their peculiar school facilities, and our Khazghi is regarded today as merely a "Native" convenience. From the evidence, and from bits and pieces of knowledge put together, I know that my people had to form some type of union, to have some deep collaboration of minds, in order to leave such a monument. This is a point not dwelled upon by most historians who wrote about early Eskimo culture. Much more was written about the oddities and exotica of Eskimo ways of life, as seen by an outsider, the "curiosities," such as nose-rubbing attributed to the Eskimo, mannerisms of individual subjects, and inaccurate generalizations about living habits.

The skinboat is also a thing of the past. It has been adapted to the new western technological age, through subtle changes of its timeless design. The most important change was the transom, which was altered to accommodate an outboard motor having a shafted extension. The mode of fastening or attaching the frame on some boats has been changed, from leather, to rawhide rope, to bolts and nuts. One of the more enduring qualities of the Umiak is its ability to hold a large amount of load, while it is light enough to be lifted by three or four strong men when empty. Also, it has a natural tendency to flex with heavy seas and large waves, the rawhide ties on the frame taking up the stresses and strains. Riding in it can be less of an experience of "shock" when the large waves do not cause the boat to rock and spank like other boats tend to do. During one of my first rides on the skinboat, I remember the way in which the movement of the water alongside of the translucent walrus hide covering fascinated me. It is very translucent when freshly put on the boat, but as time ages the skins, it tends to grow more and more opaque and discolored.

Today my father owns a thirty-three foot skinboat. But such impediments prevail as soaring walrus hide prices, crew shortage, lack of time to spend on hunting and fishing because of the need to supplement earnings, and not enough people with skills capable of working on maintenance. He is forced to utilize shortcuts, such as painting the covering with marine paint, paying exorbitant prices for hides, paying the few skilled people around Nome to repair or recover it, and using it only in the summer months when he is on vacation from his regular labors. Even more than this is involved in owning a skinboat today, because of the conditions in Nome. It is only because my father was raised in a hunting and fishing community that he holds so strongly to his traditions, and all that is implicit in providing the family with food from the natural surroundings. Even today, he incurs all expenses for the boat, but helps some of the less fortunate Nome natives by allowing them to go out in the summer hunts with him and his small crew. About five years ago, during one of these hunts, I was able to participate in a small way. Between working at various jobs, I was delighted to go with my father during week-ends, in order to supplement the crew. One especially successful hunt lasted for a week: One day preparing for the trip, four days out in the waters, and two days to process the catch and return all the gear to its proper place. During this trip I discovered the carrying capacity of a thirty-three foot skinboat. This was all common knowledge for the older men of the crew and for my father, but I was immensely impressed. Preparations for the summer hunt are carefully laid out, and involve much more than merely getting the boat ready and starting the sea hunt itself.

First, invitations are given to at least twenty persons, since invariably there are some who cannot make the trip because of other obligations. Such obligations mainly consist of summer jobs in Nome, which are precious and needed. Then, my father decides from various data if it will be good enough weather for the anticipated three or four days out. The hunt takes place in the spring, when shore ice is still clinging to the shallow two to five miles off shore along the coast. Weather conditions are important, both for the safety of the boat and crew, and for the game, which can be scarce in foul weather. On one trip, eleven men, including myself, were available. My father and I were then busy transporting the men and their gear to our camp, four miles east of Nome. After three or four trips back and forth, the men and gear are all at Fort Davis, where father has his camp and boats. Each crew member brought with him the same kinds of articles as his fellow: personal effects, extra clothing, rifles and shotguns, ammunition, binoculars, eating utensils and the like. Some of the elder men bring their native hunting paraphernalia, such as sealskin hunting bags, seal hooks (a wooden float with four hooks at its widest part, with a seal skin rope attached to its narrow end, much like an electric bulb shaped article), homemade hunting knives, seal-skin pants, special seal-skin hunting mukluks, and harpoons. Each person also brings his own food staples, enough to last at least four days. These are placed into two or three large boxes with hinged lids. A couple of campstoves, pots and pans, and a small tent are readied for the trip. The boat is pulled to the river by using planks and logs as skid blocks over the rougher terrain. Otherwise, it is easily pulled over the unmelted spring snow remaining on the ground. During April the camp grounds are still largely covered with firm, unmelted spring snow.

Once in the water, unloaded, the boat rides high on the waters, since it is so light. First, the main outboard motor is attached to the rear, a 25-horsepower "eevehjhook" is adequate for the hunt. This is the Eskimo name, the native translation for the trademark term "evinrude," one of the first types of outboard motors used at Wales. Another outboard motor of less horsepower is also loaded, as a backup motor in case of a major malfunction of the primary motor. Approximately sixty gallons of gasoline is stowed near the rear of the boat in various containers, such as five gallon cans, twenty gallon drums, and six gallon tanks for the motors.

Although the outboard motor has added greatly to the uses and functions of the skinboat, almost nothing is left to chance in preparing for the traditional skinboat hunt. On many boats today, there is still the receptacle for the sailmast on the keel. Extra pieces of walrus hide are laid down on the bottom to protect the frames and covering from loads and misplaced feet. One of the first precautions taught to novice skinboat sailors is to be watchful continually as to where one puts his feet, in order not to endanger the structural balance between frame and hide. The extra pieces of hide are also an emergency repair kit, in the event of a collision with sharp ice chunks in the open seas, or a wounded walrus charging the boat and puncturing the hide. These are materials to make a quick repair.

During this period of the loading stage, the captain is responsible for directing the placement of the initial load. He takes into consideration the weight factor of each item and also the susceptibility to water damage of any piece. Clothing and personal effects are usually loaded over the foodstuff, at the forward third section. The middle section is loaded with more bulky items, such as canvas tarpaulins, driftwood poles for shallow water maneuvering, sealskin poke floats, and other items easily moved about to make room for the anticipated game.

When the boat is finally on its way, headed for the area planned by the captain, its load is substantial enough so that the waterline is now along the chine line, and the motor has a much better hold of the waters at the aft position than if it had to push an empty boat. The captain usually has the option of changing his mind about the hunting site, if he has reason to believe that weather conditions would allow him the benefit of multiple choice, and if the original site chosen does not prove sufficiently fruitful.

During the particular hunt in which I participated, the weather was extremely favorable, the sun beating down on the ice floes, on the water, and on the faces and hands of the crew members during the mid-day hours. Everyone donned his sunglasses, which are important assets in a springtime hunt. Protection of the eyes is a major concern for the sighting of game at long distances, to note leads of open water amidst floating ice floes, and to spot any signs of impending foul weather. As proof of the sun's relentless rays, most of the crew members have faces and hands so tanned by the sun that their white parka covers contrast almost ridiculously, defying camouflage. During the two to three hour boat ride to the hunting site itself, the men complain little about the cold sea breezes, the water being at first calm and smooth as glass, protected by the huge ice floes from tidal movements. The sun offers a warm side to everything it reaches, and the labors of the preliminary loading by hand has physically warmed each crew member. The warmth lasts well into the first hours of the voyage to the hunting site, and all have a sense of the sun's comforting glow.

At this point of the venture, the older and more experienced men are noticeably elated. They are the last of a genuine Eskimo culture, which once hunted every day. This phase of the skinboat ride provides a continuing sequence of their younger days, instead of an escape from the wretched conditions of present-day Nome. A show of emotion, in their eyes, is an exaggerated theatrical production of the modern world as seen in the only movie theater of Nome, in magazines, or in other contacts with the outside world which has changed their way of life so greatly. Yet, they cannot restrain themselves from exuding a certain sense of pride and human cooperation, which overshadows all the strife they have left behind for the moment on the shores of the Seward Peninsula. This is their show; and often it is just that. Tourism is such a large economic factor for the Eskimos living in Nome, that even this very real experience has quite recently become part of the dollar sign.

Now tourists are flocking in by the hundreds during the summertime, crowding the hotels, filling up the "package" tours, and altogether contributing to the complete destruction of everything truly Eskimo.

My father is at the helm, or at the rear of the boat, in either of his usual stances, in steering the umiak through the open leads that he has reconnoitered earlier by driving to Cape Nome. He is either sitting on the very small seat, made by the joining of the two large driftwood sheer stringers atop the sides of the boat, or standing on top of it for a better view; his right hand is on the steering handle of the motor. He chooses to wear Eskimo garb over the type of clothing that I have had to be content with. I am wearing two pairs of pants over a pair of long johns, a sweater over a shirt, and the heaviest coat that I own, underneath an Army surplus Arctic overwhite. He has on a pair of sealskin pants over regular pants, and an Eskimo parka over a wool shirt. If I had to rely upon hunting for my means of existence, I too would prefer his mode of dress, since not even the Army has made much advance over the native wear, in its research and development of Arctic clothing. But my time has been spent mostly in school, which has not even bothered to mention anything about Eskimo dress in any of the teaching or school books that I and the rest of my classmates used. Naturally, I am less prepared. As another farcical recollection, I might mention that the tourists who visit Nome are furnished with a colorful facsimile of the Eskimo parka, presumably to fit in with the atmosphere. Needless to say, they are bad copies of the real thing.

My father is generally a genial-mannered man. Sitting there at the helm of his boat, however, he has the look of a supremely happy man. Occasionally, remarking on the weather conditions and experiences of past hunts to the other well-seasoned hunters, he is no longer the Janitor Working At The Nome Public Schools. For him, this is a not unhappy position, let me hasten to add, since it helps him support his family and keeps him out of the welfare rolls, which he despises as a solution for many natives who, like himself, originated from the outlying villages. He is now the functioning part of his crew. His responsibilities involve a successful and extremely important venture involving all those in the boat. No longer is his responsibility that of maintaining school facilities, with authority handed down from higher-ups; he is not pushing a broom now. He is happy, and relies less on small talk and idle jokes to make him smile. Throughout the trip, he is off on a personal interlude which brings him back to his former well-loved profession. He is unhampered for a while by the day to day events, which force him to dream of things he can only dream of. He knows too well that his lack of formal education has left him with only Social Security to look forward to when his present job demands a younger body and mind.

He keeps careful record in a diary of what has transpired up to date in the hunts, and is always careful to note the weather as a required entry. The results of a hunting expedition are entered here too. He is not an angry man, filled with envy of the white storeowners and position holders having well paid jobs in Nome. Rather, he holds great esteem for anyone who has the ability to make gains because of their intellect and resourcefulness, and he has always encouraged his three sons to get as much education as possible. He does not expect as much from his two daughters; perhaps his reticent attitude on this point stems from his desire to leave the girls to my mother for counseling. Encouragement to his boys has also largely been routed through our mother. Even before the concern for today's "generation gap" became a national issue, our family experienced the full force of a devastating cultural transition, with much more involved than one human generation.

As the seal hunting area comes in sight and is recognized by the crewmen through study of the ice conditions (such as the age of the ice as determined by surface shapes and textures), and through the landmarks and their relationships to other landmarks, the seasoned crewmen instruct the younger ones to keep an eye on the water and the ice floes for the sight of seals. We are now about five miles off the coast, and the ice floes are further apart now, with comparably smaller pieces floating around. The larger pieces may be two miles square, but there is more open water in this case and, therefore, more maneuvering space is available for hunting. When a seal is spotted, the motor is slowed down and the older men quickly decide which nearby open water will be the next "breather" for the seal. One of the things I have learned about Dad in this type of hunting is that he is an expert shot from a moving boat, especially when the boat is not fully loaded and is bouncing buoyantly over every small wave. This is a rare skill. However, he doesn't do as well from a fixed position, such as sitting on the edge of an ice floe. The water gets more and more restless now, as we go further and further out from the coast, but he does not grab his rifle at the sight of a seal. Only if the seal surfaces around the rear area of the boat will he demonstrate his abilities. Usually the older men will give the young novices a chance to try their shooting skill at this stage of the hunt, while awaiting the more desirable animals such as the bearded seal and walrus. These larger mammals feed further out and are to be found less frequently closer in.

If the number of seals warrants a stay around the initial contact area of the first one spotted, the captain and crew may elect to land on a good solid floe by nosing the craft in at a lower stretch of the floe's edge. The front man, who is responsible also for the harpoon, jumps out before the bow bumps the ice, and cushions the impact while also testing the strength and condition of the landing site. He then runs yards up, and holds fast with a rope. The next man steadies the boat while the rest file out. Dad remains aboard, and watches the motor's lower unit while the rest pull the bow up onto the ice ledge. A few coordinated pulls brings the boat halfway out of the water. Then the combined weight of the men leaning on the front raises the stern out of the water. The men pull forward again, bringing the boat to rest on a suitable even plane of snow and ice. Paddles are used to keep the boat upright by tying the shanks to the sides. Lunch is then served. Coffee and tea brewed on the campstove, and pilot bread finishes off the menu of dried meats and fish. If a seal is shot near the landing place, it is quickly retrieved either by a small plywood scow, or with the traditional seal hook. It is then dressed on the ice, where sea gulls get their treat of the discarded parts of the viscera. Killing of the more prized spotted seal or the bearded seals is a more complicated process, since they tend to sink as soon as they expire. The younger

THREE USES OF WHOLE SEAL BAGS

As a food container,
inverted like a wine bag.

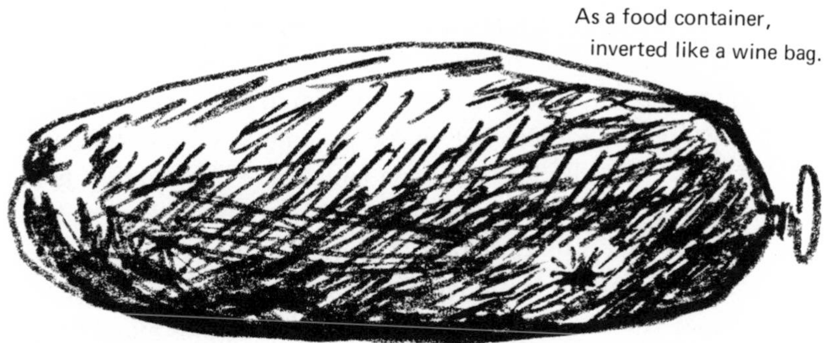

The seal is carefully skinned. Great care is taken in making this article, as it may be passed on from one generation to another as an heirloom, and usually is.

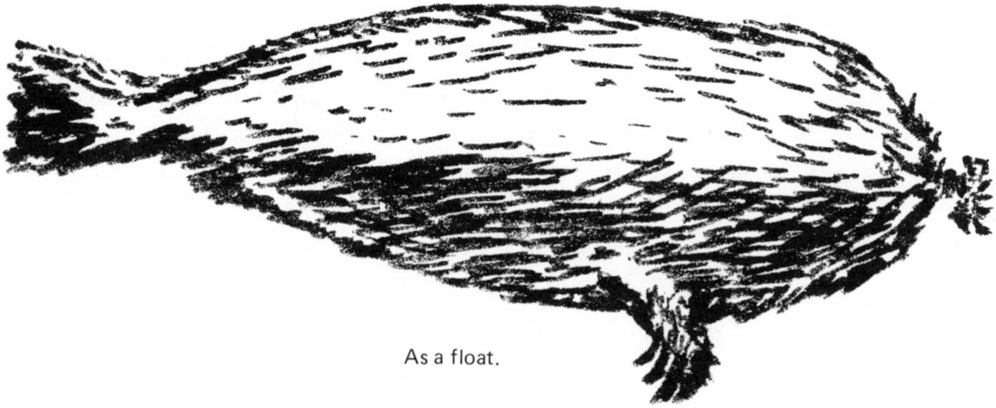

As a float.

As a hunting bag.

bearded seal sometimes refloat after an interval of about a half hour, but still it is much easier to get them while they are lying on top of the ice, or while the boat is in the water. The harpooner can then combine his skills with the rest of the crew, who must direct the boat to a favorable position for him to lance the animal.

Getting to sleep out on the sea and ice is an ordeal, as I have found. Especially for the young and eager. The sun does not lower itself for very long during the spring, and the chance to realize a catch is hard to turn down while the experienced hunters are willing to turn in and reserve their strength for the next day. So the younger men sit and watch that ever-fluctuating movement of the ice floes. I have never heard of any Eskimo crew getting caught between ice floes, often the floes move together to form pressure ridges that may reach heights of fifty feet, from ice sheets three feet thick. I have heard of boat crews finding it necessary to physically pull the boat across the top of ice floes when the closing of the open leads proves too fast for them to escape being crushed between the floes. I think the main reason is that the sea and ice, which give the Eskimo his food source, also shows its combined powers so dramatically that respect for it is gained very soon. The noise of this force is heard unceasingly. When it is nearby, I feel like a midget only inches tall, standing near a gigantic door opening and closing with very rusty hinges, so that any minute the whole doorway might give way, and slamming down hard, crack the peaceful floe I am standing on. I also fear sleeping on the ice, because waking up during the cold mornings is not the most pleasant feeling to experience. The body temperature has lowered so much in its functioning organs due to the need to rest after the hard work of the previous day. The cold air that slowly passed in and out of the lungs while asleep makes awakening like being splashed with cold water while one is nearly freezing to death. The older men stoicly bear this excruciating greeting of the early morning, and calmly ask the watch how things are. I have seen some men awaken and immediately perform some very interesting calisthenics because their limbs are stiff and almost immobile from the cramped position of sleeping in the tiny space inside the boat.

I don't think any one can fully appreciate the good taste of hot coffee, or any other hot drink, until he has had such an experience. During this particular hunting trip, we were out at sea four days, and the companionship brought about by the trip did much to teach me about the old ways in which my forefathers lived. True, many of the old ways are lost through the use of modern conveniences such as motors, campstoves and tents. But at least I have experienced in part that which my father wanted me to taste. To have a swig of it and swish it around the palate of my generation, and make my own opinion as to its worth, is a priceless gift for which I have to thank my father. Having met so many self-styled "conservationists" of wildlife, I side with the people who still hunt for a living even if it is only part time. It is a difficult way to make a living, but so is moving to Nome, for instance, from an outlying village, with the purpose of earning a living, without first being assured of a decent job.

Some of my father's crew members were well known in Nome for their alcoholic tragedies and their inability to hold a job. Others are fortunate enough to have a job of small position with little promise. They are all part of a Nome which exists essentially on the basis of keeping the status quo. Even today there are very few Eskimos living in Nome who can look forward to any future other than trying to stay alive in persistently bad housing facilities, poor sanitation conditions; and having to contend with inept and bureaucratic welfare administrations. There are many who give up, and escape to alcoholism, with the resultant destruction of families adding to the general mish-mash of federal, state and city-bred "solutions." From experience, I can reveal that these solutions do not upset the status quo.

There are conservationists who care about the wilful destruction of wildlife and natural resources. But I believe that the other (foreign) type of hunting in Alaska is definitely sinful. At least, they are opposed to the laws of nature.

Those who come to Alaska on trophy-hunting expeditions should be stopped before they start. An example is Kotzebue, where polar bears are hunted for a costly proof of one's daring and adventurous spirit. The bears are shot down after chasing them from light planes equipped with skis. The profits are made by those who can afford light planes, not by the native people, whom I regard as the truly adventurous and daring ones, as compared to the white hunter with elephant gun, movie camera, and the guarantee of a kill.

Perhaps, on the other hand, in some way, conservation and prevention of "wilful and careless destruction of wildlife and natural resources" might also be made to apply to the Alaskan natives?

After the four days' hunt, we returned to Fort Davis, possessing everything we started out with, minus some of the food and ammunition expended on the game, four full grown oogruk or bearded seal with an average size of twelve feet long, four young oogruk measuring seven feet, five spotted seals seven feet long but slimmer than young oogruk, four ribbon seals five feet long, and eleven common seals varying in size from four to five feet long. They filled up the entire middle section of the boat: Twenty-eight seals and eleven men with gear, tired but contented, were quietly greeted on that memorable afternoon, by the wives and children. Again I felt that glowing sense of pride in the community effort that ties this disappearing Eskimo way of life to the past. And I thought: How fortunate I am to be the son of Willie Senungetuk!

This episode passed by without any real effect upon the economy of Nome and its constituency of business men. In fact, no one except the crew members and their families knew about it. Indirectly, the tourists know the surface part of certain aspects of Native life, and indeed have it recorded on film. They pay the airlines responsible for transporting them to Nome to do the filming. I am sure my father felt as I did after that hunt. I am certain he felt my pride in him. He must have understood the deep, unspoken thanks from the crew members and their families, who were able to feed themselves for a little while without having to fill out welfare forms or to labor for the almighty dollar.

7

Climate and Food

It is somehow amazing if not amusing, to find that so many misconceptions still exist about Alaska, and particularly about its climate. Many people still believe that the Far North is a "miserably cold place, inhospitable, of continuing frozen winters." There are, in fact, distinct seasonal changes in the Alaska region.

It can generally be said that the winters are indeed cold, lasting usually from the end of October until the month of March. The spring season starts in Wales, for example, around April, gathering its full impetus in May and spreading into summer in June. Each day has its own personality, no two days apparently of the same duration. The short summer months of June, July and August bring forth a season of intermittent wind and sunshine, with little rain. Then, the fall of the year appears, with more wind, and rains. October is the month when the huge soft snowflakes are falling, landing on the hard ground, making ready for the months of winter, which again give way to the fresh spring season with all its joys and surprises. Truly a land of beautiful variety!

Spring is that time of the year having most to offer the Native for his food. In Wales, the dead of winter still provides a season for obtaining fresh meat. These are the owl, (rarely eaten at other times), the ptarmigan, jack rabbits from the land, seals and fish from the sea. Of course, stored foods from the previous spring and summer were also available. But the main winter-time fish, dependably available, were the small cod, crab, and the flounder. Crab was always cooked before eaten. But the cod and flounder were sometimes eaten after having been previously frozen in the sheds until ready for serving. When thawed, they are back again to a true "raw" state, with certain changes making them very palatable and delicious.

To explain this, let me offer a new word: *Koowahk*. This is actually an old Eskimo word, meaning *meat in a frozen state,* having ice crystals between the layers of muscle, so that there is a separation between water and meat. Also, I shall extend the descriptive range usually ascribed to the various ways in which meat may be prepared, from "raw," and "cooked," to still another state . . . *Koowahk*. After all, "raw" and "cooked" encompasses merely the food habits only of *some* areas of the world. Frozen meat or fish has already undergone a change in texture and palatability. We could then make a distinction between (1) Koowahk (frozen), (2) Raw (thawed), and (3) Cooked. I believe this is a somewhat more sophisticated description than the western man's simple distinction between raw or cooked foods.

What was man's reason for inventing heat in order to change meats and other foods from the raw to the cooked state? Taste. Does the Eskimo enjoy tasty foods better than so-so food? Yes, In his earlier cultural period, did the Eskimo have access to heat? Not very much. Some driftwood, animal fats, and moss. In the winter, did he have access to cold places where he could alter the taste of his food? Yes. In the summer, too? No. What did he then do to make his foods, principally meats, more tasty? He dried them, cooked them, and cured them; sometimes he smoked them.

The Koowahk was not eaten by itself, as some picture books sold to tourists might portray. Each person at the table was given a finger dish, containing a couple of ounces of seal oil. With sharp knives and ulus, taking care not to handle the Koowahk too long with warm hands, the fish or meat was sliced into thin strips and then dipped into the seal oil, before savoring the combined flavors of oil and frozen meat. An ulu is an Eskimo knife usually more specifically called an Eskimo woman's knife. It is shaped like a triangle with point up, and the other two points rounded out to form an almost circular cutting edge, where the base of the triangle would be. The handle, often ornately carved, is attached to the top

Two types of ulus: Utilitarian (right) and ornate.

Hunting knife with ivory handle.

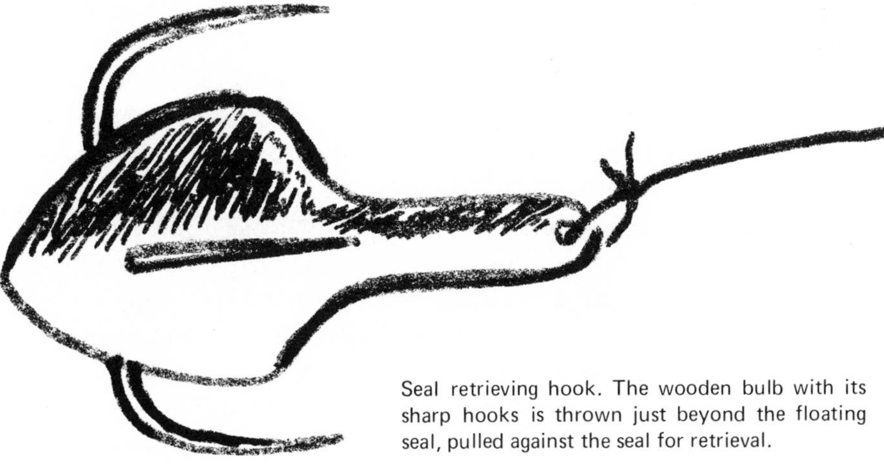

Seal retrieving hook. The wooden bulb with its sharp hooks is thrown just beyond the floating seal, pulled against the seal for retrieval.

point. Its size varies with the smallest ones (with a two-inch cutting edge), usually used as utilitarian toys; and the largest ones (with a nine-inch cutting edge), for heavy work, such as splitting walrus hides for skinboats. There was no real hurry to keep the bite-sized meat from melting in the mouth and losing that special favor gained from Koowahking. It does not melt that fast. Any one who has tried to melt an ice cube rapidly in the mouth should know. Besides, does one hurry when eating ice cream or sherbet?

Although Koowahk was served occasionally in the winter, there were other ways of preparing foods. Tom cods, and a smaller, tastier variety of cod were the most plentiful, along with the lowly bullhead. These were prepared in many different ways: boiling for meat and soup, hanging outside in the clean northern air for drying just before cooking, intensive drying, frying, baking, and adding to it the *Kamahmuk*, or Reindeer tallow and seal oil — a mixture having an appearance very much like cottage cheese.

Only the flounder was not as adaptable to ways of preparation because of its unique taste as Koowahk. The Wales off-shore flounder measured anywhere from three inches to seven or eight inches. In its frozen state, it was easily served at the dinner table. The ulu, or Eskimo woman's knife, was run over it for slicing, in a sort of rocking motion.

The technology of catching the flounder is one of the most artful forms of fishing in the world. First, the flounder fishing spot is given extra attention. More than, say, a Tom Cod fishing hole. The flounder fishing spot is about three-quarters of a mile out, in one certain place of the Wales village shore, possibly because the smaller crustacian are found there in the summer. A snow shelter is made by piling pressure ridge ice chunks in a horseshoe shaped wall around the fishing hole. It is about four feet high. The fishing equipment consists of: a small sled, a burlap bag or two, a length of cord, an ice chisel, a fishing hole ice skimmer, a fishing line with an ivory lure, and the flounder spear. And, warm clothing.

The fisherman lays stomach down, with feet towards the open part of the horseshoe-shaped ice wall. The hole is at the other end, well protected by the walls of ice. The fishing line, or jigger, is held in the left hand, with the arm circumscribing the hood ruff. I have a feeling that the woman's wide wolf hood ruff had a good purpose before it became a fashion symbol for the well-dressed Eskimo lady. A wide ruff makes it easier to cut reflections in the hole, so that the ocean floor is more visible. The right hand holds the flounder spear, with its barbs submerged in a ready position. It is not deep waters where the flounders are. The left hand jiggles the lure and the flounder is seen curiously undulating towards the lure, stopping now and then, as all game fish are not completely gullible. The good flounder fisher knows how to make the lure act alive. When the flounder sees the descending barbs, it is quick to move away, so the fisherman also must be quick. The shelter is used both for eliminating glare and to keep the wind out. The sled can sometimes hold two bags of flounder from a single day's fishing.

One should remember that some of the fishing gear described above was brought to the Eskimo by western man, at a time when European instruments and innovations were still being peacefully utilized as additions to Eskimo life, without the European over-running Eskimo culture and degrading Eskimo lifeways and Native technology. Modern gear includes the ice chisel blade, the burlap bags, the cord and the steel runners of the sled.

Indeed, considering the general misconception that Eskimo people had little choice of foods, it is surprising to many that there was considerable variety in the diet. There are various types of seals around the Nome area, for example. Some are tastier than others. Fried seal liver surpasses any other type of animal liver available in stores. Dried fish, hung on driftwood racks in the fishing camps, does not cause spoilage, but actually preserves the fish, so that it can be kept for a long time, and is used extensively as a staple during the long skinboat hunting expeditions. Different kinds of berries and other wild plants are gathered, and prepared in many different ways. *Ush shak* is the fermented flippers of the seal or walrus. Its taste is similar to that of the *Muk tuk* of the whale, which has been described by non-Eskimos as akin to the taste of almonds in olive oil. Muk tuk is the layer of whale skin, which includes about an inch of fat, and about three-quarters of an inch of black rubbery skin. The very outer layer of the muk tuk is scraped off, so in truth the epidermis of the whale is not eaten. But,

Ush shak, or *Muk tuk* are not everyday dietary treats today. For one thing, *Muk tuk* is prohibitively expensive when purchased at the stores — about $3.50 per pound. *Ush shak* cannot be made in the old Eskimo way without utilization of the underground storage cellars, which are not readily available in Nome and other towns of Alaska. My father has made a *Saluk,* or underground storage area, near his fishing camp. It really doesn't have the same permafrost surroundings so necessary for this type of preparatory storage, which our Wales village storage cellar had.

Some diarists and historians have described the climate of Northern Alaska as unbearably cold. At the same time, they have described the Eskimos as enjoying "rotten food." This is certainly a contradiction. In a climate which does not readily turn all meats into inedible spoiled garbage, as would occur in some parts of the Lower-Forty-Eight, the Eskimos must try very hard to get their meats to "cure", or "age", which is what I suppose the foreigners mean when they describe *rotten* food. What indeed are pickled, aged, cured, kippered, or smoked foods! These are served as tasty hors d'oeuvres. To me and my people, these are "rotten foods." Here again there is a difference in understanding, a misconception due to the use of a word with adverse connotations, and a readiness to ascribe negative qualities to any people whose ways may seem "strange," or different.

It is quite true that one needs to acquire a taste for Eskimo foods. But, on the other hand, so did I have to acquire a taste for the American hot dog, which tasted to me like rubber laced with condiments, when I first had it. In Nome, where many whites associated with the Natives, usually either through intermarriage, or friendships, quite a few non-Natives have acquired a taste for Eskimo food. This happens not only in an Eskimo, mixed-blood, white community, such as Nome, but also in the outlying villages, where teachers, weather bureau station managers, missionaries, and construction workers have a closer contact with the people and their Native foods. Indeed, the villages will tend to measure the friendliness of an outsider by his willingness to *Nay pew ruk* or, "taste a little."

There are many Native Alaskan foods which are rapidly disappearing as a cultural habit. First of all, because of the introduction of commodities that are supposedly more "civilized." Certainly they are not more nutritional. Another important aspect is that the young Eskimos are immediately introduced to grocery-store foods and farm-grown produce. Other economic factors enter into this picture. Take the reindeer. The two reindeer herders in Nome today find it difficult to supply the Eskimo meat buyer alone, when other countries such as Japan and Korea, show considerable interest in importing reindeer meat products to their countries, at lucrative prices. However, the U. S. Department of the Interior and the Food and Drug Administration do not yet consider the reindeer industry as a possible American resource for international trade. Japan has found a ready source for herring roe from Southeast Alaska. Korea is interested in the alleged aphrodisiac qualities of the reindeer horn. The reindeer herders in Nome do a satisfactory business with the Alaskan Eskimo buyers. They have had some help from the U.S. Government in the management of their internal business problems, but they are hampered because of the lack of sufficient government meat packers' examining stations. Thus, they cannot pursue far-reaching plans for growth.

The reindeer were first imported into Alaska to introduce a new and natural business opportunity for Native Alaskans. But there are problems. Due to the feeding habits of the reindeer, they are subjected to radiation because they feed on the moss and lichen of Alaska. The plants are non-seasonal in their growing stages. They collect radiation resulting from the fallout of nuclear testing by the United States and Russia before the ban. The reindeer, in turn, eat the moss and lichen, and themselves build up the radiation in their bodies.

Native Eskimo foods are disappearing from their economy, because of western man's education of the young Eskimo. Certainly, they do not learn in school anything about the old ways of preparing Eskimo foods. Add to this factor, the ideas instilled in the young Natives that if it is a White American meal, it must be good. Since it finds acceptance among the majority of the country's population, it sets the young Native apart if he insists upon his own Native foods. They simply want to be "with it," accepting the foreigners' ways, turning away from their own Native foods, if offered by the elders.

The Innupiat belonged in a very real sense to a group of people who relied on collective gathering of plants and animals, and wastefulness was not a part of their lives. The old saying, "Everything used except the squeal," applied to the main item of food, particularly the seal. Eskimo hunters had to know a good deal about anatomy in order to successfully butcher the animal so that all parts were properly readied for cooking or storage. Even the bones were either fed to the dogs or made into toys for the children. If any uninformed white person gags at this, let him think of the uses of ivory, sealskin fur coats, whalebone corset stays, and the use of an elk tooth as a symbol hung around the neck by members of the fraternal group called the B.P.O.E.

I can remember that the knuckle bones of the seal were used much like dice in some favorite games. Their position after the throw was calculated for points. This was not a gambling game, but one in which the players had to figure for completion of a story, a hunting story, whether successful or not. A part of the arm bone was used for a game of skill. The bone was tied to a string attached to an ivory rod, and the contestant had to try to swing the bone up in the air and catch it by one of two foramina as it fell. One of the holes was more difficult to spear, consequently it was named the boys' challenge, and the easier one the girls'.

Hunting, gathering, food preparation and storage, games invented thousands of years ago, and the economic and social system that was a part of our daily lives did not deserve to be smashed. Far better to have taken the best of both, and constructed a way of life much more satisfying and rewarding than what we have today.

8

Our World in Transition

In Wales, the possessions accumulated from the white man's manufacture were much treasured by Willie, few as they were. The house we lived in was made of ship-lap and two-by-fours, with heavier planking for flooring. These were certainly manufactured or processed outside of Alaska, as were the nails to put all of it together. However, nails and finished wood were very hard to come by, and nails were used sparingly and often re-used from other sources.

The immediate vicinity of our house contained the necessary grounds to hold my father's material wealth. The living area was comprised of the main room, about ten by fourteen feet, the adjacent storage room with a lower roof but with the same amount of floor space, and a small storm shed. This was the extent of our modest living quarters until 1945. During that year, my father built another addition to the house, another large room to be used for storage, in front of the entire house. He left the small storm shed in place, since he could not decide what to use it for if he took it apart. Besides, it would help keep the main living room warm. There was only one stove in the house, a wood burning stove set square in the middle of the side wall of the main room. Behind it were a couple of shelves used to dry mukluks, mittens, and socks. Other supplies for the hunter were either put into bags and left in the main room, or stored in either of the two large storage rooms together with other hunting and fishing gear.

Dad built the front storage room with lumber he had collected from various places during a couple of years. The main provider of the two-by-fours, the one-by-sixes, and several other odd-sized lumber was the beach. During his walks in the summertime, he gathered finished lumber which had been delivered by the winds, currents, and the tidal action, and made neat stockpiles near the beach, where he would remember to take his dog sled. As soon as winter snows made it possible to sled them, he brought them to our house. With utmost patience he waited until the next year when the wood dried out and the summertime again made it possible to repeat the process. After two summers of waiting, and much work to gather the lumber, he was ready to construct the addition to the house. He could only find four windows from the village store, so he made the frame with only two smallish window spaces. A hand saw, one or two hammers, a square, and a few other tools he had accumulated had to suffice as tools with which to build the addition, all in one summer's labor. Or else, he knew that the winter snows would build up around the house so much that the incomplete structure would not be able to support the snow drifts that pile up at Wales.

The summer walks were not only for the purpose of gathering wood, both for building and for burning. They were also for setting fish nets, to hunt for eggs and ducks, to gather dried grass for boot insulation, and for Dad's temporary line of work: taking care of the claims of the outsider's prospecting ventures. At one time, he also had a part in the not too successful reindeer herding cooperative in Wales. This took a lot of walking in order to keep up with the herd. Therefore the Wales men, with all of their other obligations, could not make a success of a project that needed constant attention. Other villagers in various Eskimo settlements have also been only partly successful, and they still have some reindeer which were at first imported from the Scandinavian countries. They are making some profit from the venture now. Wales was not close enough to a market to stimulate the growth of a herd. Villages closer to Nome have had a small market from the town itself and from its outlying villages.

In fact, walking alone out of the village at Wales was not done very often during the summer. Since much of the hunting was a collective affair during the spring, the men had a limited amount of spare time. Thus, only after the big hunts of the spring did they feel free to do the things they might want to do on their own. My father and his brother once set up an Eskimo type house about twelve miles up the coast, using driftwood from the adjacent beach. I have never really been clear as to the purpose of this large undertaking. I mean, it seems apparent that it would be a summer-type camp area, which would enable the brothers to stay close to the hunting and fishing grounds. Animals will not linger around an area constantly inhabited by man. Over a period of years they will move their migratory routes to compensate for the intrusions. The Wales area, which is peopled, is no longer a haven for anything except dumb clams and fish, such as the Tom Cod and the Beach Flounder. Thus, it is entirely possible that Willie and his brother, Andrew, wanted a place to call their own — for use as a rest area when passing by during the winter, and as a campsite during the summer. Certainly the hunter, after working most of the short winter day, will be happy to stop midway between the hunting area and home for a hot cup of tea. The dogs, too, welcome a chance to rest before their run home. No matter how tired they may be after a long day's work, especially when hauling a good catch, the dogs will always speed up during the last miles towards home.

If there are any who cannot make "the home run," usually a young practicing pup, they are given a free ride home. It was not unusual to see Dad come home lickety-split on a dog sled hauling two or three seals, his hunting bag, ice testing pole, rifles, grub box, extra clothing, and a pathetic looking young dog with bloody feet, tied snugly to the bouncing sled.

The symphony or the cacophony, whichever way a person feels about the noise of a villageful of dogs, always accompanied arrival of a hunter, the dogs sounding as if they were terribly jealous of the incoming team. It was a certain way of announcing the arrival of any of the neighbors' hunting parties, since the poorly insulated houses enabled the occupants to listen to the special kinds of barking and howling around the neighborhood. If this reached full resonance and excitement from the dogs still at their chains, somebody would be elected to go outside the house and check to see if the men had come home. Even when the person elected for this happy chore did not at once return inside, the ensuing noises would tell the rest of the family that indeed the daily hunt was over with and a night of replacing dogs and equipment was in store for the older boys. The women would have to ready space for the catch. One learned how to translate the sounds of the dogs also. Some dogs had such easily identifiable voices that one could not mistake him for another. Or her. Although rarely, it happens sometimes that the leader of the dog team will be a female dog. Dad had one very memorable female dog, who proved to be a great leader, a family pet, and his true companion on lonely hunting trips.

Her name was "Cake," one of the names given to a dog signifying nothing but a new western culture item, a thing of modern convenience which was not often tasted in Wales. "Cake" was trusted to lead the team, she recognized dangerous ice conditions, took the smoothest routes to and from the hunting grounds, worked the hardest when asked to, and played when given the chance. Many of the now yellowed photographs scattered about at home show "Cake" in a reclining position with her head held up high, one of many dogs who without question match or surpass the much-publicized "Lassies" of the television world. Only the family knows these wonderful dogs. They have left this world quietly, with the fondest memories in the hearts of the masters. With the advent of the motorized snowmobiles, even the memories will be erased from tomorrow's Eskimos.

In the winter, the dog trails followed the beach, with slight deviation to account for the different types of terrain near the sea, and distances involving shortcuts when the land jutted outwards as flat and smooth tundra. The main trails were further branched out, with individual trails to individual hunting areas. One branch may go to a private seal-netting hole, or to another place for fishing, and still another for traveling to the edge of the shore ice to shoot seal on different days. If one area did not prove fruitful enough, the hunter might decide to move on to another. This was one of Dad's characteristics, as I came to discover during the years I spent with him and his crew at Nome. He would rather move to another spot than spend the day waiting for his moment of truth in one place, even if other well seasoned Nome area hunters remained and waited longer for the right time of day, the right winds, and the right currents. It does take an enormous lot of patience to outwit animals, especially if they are adapted to a totally different environment, such as the sea. Even if one knows he is in the vicinity of the waterways of the type of seal he is hunting, he must be able to figure the direction of travel by the first sighting of the seal, if it is too far out to shoot. Then he must be ready for the next breaching to sight the rifle accurately. The distance must be instantly calculated, the windage compensated for, and the decision to pull the trigger must be made in case the seal proves to be too inaccessible due either to distance or barriers such as strong currents, ice separation, ice conditions, or lack of retrieving gear. I am relating these problems in usage of the rifle since I cannot visualize *not* having a rifle to hunt with, even though it was done for centuries through time immemorial. Without a rifle, the hunter must have had to maintain his hunting spirit on the tip of a chilly, miserable place for hours, not quite sure if all that bother was going to feed the family the next day. Having to rely totally on the tip of sharpened bone or rock tied to wood, the pre-rifle Eskimo had to be sure of his skills. One thinks of the times this old-time hunter must have spent practicing with his elders, not wanting to be known as a failure. One imagines how his mind must have been tightly wound as a trigger mechanism, ready to act out what had made him survive. And now, after all this, he is put down by Mother Invention. That which has made his hunting so much easier has also made it more difficult for him to realize his true worth, considering all that the rifle has brought with it.

A valued article of attire was made of the skins of various birds. But in Wales, by the time of my generation, the use of bird skins had disappeared. I have heard of some earlier, very wealthy men who wore such exotic parkas as Eider duck head, and neck skins. Or the skin of dried salmon. For a short time, when I was a child, we small tots were encouraged, probably more as a pastime than for actual usefulness, to save the Eider duck head, the neck and back skins. The avowed purpose was to build up a supply of these items for a future wealthy man's parka. Of course, none was ever made, and the skins were eventually thrown away, since it probably took more knowledge than we had to treat the bird skins for sewing. My father did have the walrus intestine water-proof overdress, and it was only used during a short rainy season in the fall. By this time, there were no kayaks left. Now there are the commercial places where one can obtain regular raincoats which are easier to take care of.

The scalloped style for the parka was never used in Wales, at least during my time. Also, hides of the bear, the fox, mink and fawn were not extensively used. The fox was already fairly well depleted by virtue of its short-lived popularity in the Lower-Forty-Eight. Squirrel skins were used more often, and the "fancy parka" which my mother yearned to have for so long she did not make until we had moved to Nome. She had already acquired quite a few squirrel skins, but she needed more. A "fancy parka" used only the choice belly parts of the animal. Mom's parka has for decoration white calfskin in front near the shoulders, white and black calfskin checks there, and on the sleeves and hem, wolverine tassels on the back of the shoulders, in front and upon the shoulders, beaver skin on the cuffs, a wolf ruff around the hood, and beads on the sides of the hood. It was made with special care, and she still treasures it as much as any White woman socialite would treasure her mink coat. Also, she can re-work it if she gets better-looking fur. For example, she has changed the ruff a couple of times, whenever she had the good fortune to acquire better quality wolf fur . . . very much like ordering parts to customize a car! Whatever parts she exchanged go to other "everyday" parkas. The use of calf and beaver skin was probably started after some traders introduced various other furs in exchange for more marketable ones.

The whole of life in my Native village was like another world . . . a world of our own. Transportation, communication, obtaining food and clothing, the economics of life itself, were so much simpler and so much richer. That is the way it seems to me now.

We had one type of sport, principally played by the King Island children. This involved the use of polar bear skin. The skin was cleaned in a way that brought both fun and practicability to our lives, through the simple method of allowing us to use the bear skin as a sled. This permits the snow itself to clean the oils and stains from the skin. Running downhill on a polar bearskin is a very fast and sometimes even a dangerous sport. I can remember one ride on such a vehicle, disclosing the fact that not many polar bears roamed around Wales. There was the added difficulty of bringing one down, even if it was spotted by the hunter.

The King Islanders had greater opportunity to become adept in hunting the polar bear, naturally. Since they lived further out at sea, and there was a quantity of bears in their area, they developed a special system of hunting the animal. This necessitated the special use of dogs, something that the "flatland" mainlanders did not train their dogs to do. The King Island dogs were trained to follow the fast moving polar bear, and head it towards the team of hunters. If it could not be directed to the hunting team, the dogs at least harassed the animal enough to slow it down. One story of a King Island polar bear hunt was told to me by my friend, Pete Seeganna, a young man close to my own age. It remained in his memory for its comical situation as well as for the memorable adventure that it was, as in any big game hunt. Here is Pete's story:

Five hunters, including Pete as an apprentice of sorts, were out on the ice with four dogs after having sighted the bear through strong binoculars from the high lookout point on King Island. This was when a polar bear had not been sighted for a long period of time. The men were eager to catch the "Nanook," knowing that its meat would be a pleasant change from fish and small game. They trekked out as rapidly as possible with their hunting clothes on, and soon started to sweat and breathe hard. The weak, oblique heat of the sun did not cause surplus body warmth but the colder temperatures atop the ice were not uncomfortable. As soon as the bear was at a distance that made trailing it relatively easier, with the consequent possibility of success, adrenaline flowed, and one of the men threw off his parka. He knew he could retrieve it afterwards by backtracking. The dogs were ahead, filled with the same spirit of impending contact with the wary white inhabitant of the snow, ice and water. The slow-motion strides of the running bear compared to ten fast steps for the men and five blurry gallops for the dogs, was a re-enactment of the ages-old King Island polar bear hunt. The bear's rump, as seen by the hunters, rose and fell like a huge oval-shaped snowball rolling down a white rocky slope. Occasionally it would rear up its head with its very black nose, to see what sort of creatures would have the audacity to run lickety-split behind him. He was making a tremendous effort to lose the hunters, and be left alone to do his own hunting. Every time he stopped, the men tried harder to lessen the distance between themselves and the bear.

So the chase went on, the men feeling sometimes as if their lungs would burst, if they surrendered to exhaustion. They knew they would be defeated, if they allowed this to happen. At last the ice chunks, as large as Volkswagens, were grouped closer together, due to a pressure ridge over another group of pressure ridges, the chunks looking like a junk yard for all-white Cadillacs, with clear, ice-blue trims. The dogs were beginning to realize an advantage, scrambling around over and through the rugged ice blocks, with their bases padded from unpredictable hardness or softness of snow.

The bear showed signs of pique. He considers facing the irritation of the hunt with his other defenses besides those of mobility. Many faithful dogs have sacrificed their lives, so that their masters can catch the polar bear. By this time, the men are getting ready to kneel down in the snow and try to wound the bear with quick shots, trying hard not to accidentally hit the dogs. But they don't all go down to shoot.

So far, Pete has been explaining the polar bear hunt as one hunter would tell a hunting yarn to another. Now, as Pete continues, it is as though he is still out on the ice. His hands move in quick gestures. His speech shows more and more excitement.

"There I was," said Pete, "not one of the faster runners, lagging behind just enough to watch what was going on. The one who had thrown off his parka is now leading the men. He is running as fast as his legs can go. The wind is now facing us. This man is still wearing his baseball cap that he had on under the parka. His forward momentum combines with the wind, *and the cap blows back.* He screeches to a halt. The rest of us are still running. We are catching up with him. We pass him. As I look back, he is running full speed in the opposite direction! Chasing his damned cap!! I have to stop and laugh . . . the other men keep going, and soon they have wounded the bear."

We laughed together, my friend Pete and I, at the ludicrous vision conjured up by this tale of the polar bear hunt. But sadness lay within the laughter. The uninhibited friendships of the people, whether hunting or relaxing, in fun or sorrow, will be difficult to recapture.

9

Eh Sah Ne: Taboo

Much has been written about the "character and disposition" of the Eskimo. For example, in the *Handbook of American Indians North of Mexico* (Bulletin 30, Smithsonian Institution), the section on the Eskimo states: ". . . the Eskimo may be described as peaceable, cheerful, truthful, and honest, but exceptionally loose in sexual morality." The writer does not explain which "morality" he has described: Christian, Muslim, Buddhist, Judaic, Atheist, Communist, Capitalist, or Fascist?

I think morality differs with each of these beliefs and each of the social systems which they reflect. In some reports on the Eskimo of Greenland, the early Eskimo was believed to be very liberal in matters pertaining to sex. A custom like wife-swapping was considered an immoral act by those who first visited Eskimo areas. A reader of these reports may be a little aghast at customs which are no longer part of the unique Eskimo traditions. On the other hand, the divorce and abortion laws of American society certainly cannot be said to be the products of a sexually liberal society. Indeed the present changes advocated by many in order to liberalize the laws are not far from the unwritten traditions of the Eskimo society centuries ago.

It seems to me that the Eskimo had simply adjusted to the needs of his culture and his economy. It is true that monogamy, polygamy, and polyandry were all practices which the early Eskimo had. So did all of Mankind at various stages of development. But there were no such things among us as a "lonely hearts club," newspaper advertisement personals, alimonies, broken families, prostitution or child abuse. The unwritten law was that a man could have as many wives as he could support by his hunting skills. Or, a woman could have as many husbands as she could clothe and prepare food for. In some cases, in which wife swapping was indignantly reported by righteous monogamists, the situation could well have been that a man needed to leave his village for another village, to follow the migration of game, and could not bring his wife. Here an unwritten law took effect, that of inducing a consenting husband to allow his wife to go along, so that a woman would be able to furnish companionship and wifely duties, such as keeping his clothes mended and dry while he hunted. This was strictly for the sake of convenience, and not for sexual novelty or entertainment. The whole matter of "convenience," so lightly taken by modern man, was one of life and death for the early Eskimo people.

These pre-white Eskimo practices, whether they be immoral or not according to Christian standards, are not discussed by my parents. Whatever has been associated with the Eskimo culture has been referred to by them as "Eh sah ne tuk," or translated roughly, "That which belongs to a time long ago." This term might be descriptive of anything that is not absolutely necessary for contemporary Eskimo living. Customs and traditions that might have been part of the culture a hundred years before the first European Christian was seen in Wales. Much of the Shaman, or medicine man stories, belong to *Eh sah ne.* So does anything which deals with Eskimo morality in any way not connected with present Christian dogma. Still, I see that other attributes described by the white man as Eskimo characteristics, are still retained by many Eskimos. Such as being "peaceable, cheerful, truthful, and honest." Even under present conditions, I know very few who are not of this disposition. Perhaps it is because these traits have not been criticized by the dominant culture, and the Eskimo has not yet learned to meet hardship with anger.

Also, I feel that the white man has always tended to compare his own culture with others, in a fashion such as he needs to make his own seem reasonable and civilized. I see this in the descriptions of artifacts, skull shapes, customs. Would it not be just as reasonable to compare the white skull, with the Eskimo skull, instead of the other way around? In the Report of the Commissioner of Indian Affairs for 1888, the superintendent of the Sitka, Alaska, boarding school states:

> "Our Chaplain, Rev. A.E. Austin, has labored faithfully among the native here for nine years. Christianity is a powerful lever in influencing them to abandon their old customs and in strengthening them to live above the contaminating and debasing habits which destroy both body and soul and which are rapidly depopulating the race."

This approach is one still taken by many non-Alaskan educators, and so the 1888-type thinking still prevails. Such an approach was one held by most Bureau of Indian Affairs teachers and administrators in years past. It persists among many today. There are a few scattered reports done by anthropologists and others, attempting to describe the Eskimo child. One such report, by Ales Hrdlicka (1941 Smithsonian Report), disputed earlier beliefs that the Eskimo woman did not rear her children well. According to Hrdlicka, this misconception is probably due to the high rate of infant mortality during the times when early reporters wrote, and even during more recent times. However, the writer went on to say that the young did not seem to bother to attend dances and singing done by their elders; they had no interest in Eskimo social gatherings. As an Eskimo boy raised in a small village, I cannot agree. Much of the singing and dancing among us was subtly but firmly directed to the young. There were even some "practice" songs, used to initiate boys and girls of five or six years of age into the art of dancing and singing. Usually, one or two children of the leading families were taught individually by parents at home. When a celebration was held, these children were asked to start the events, so that their peers could follow them. However, each child was allowed to progress or not, as he wished. In this way, those who were taught by their parents naturally pursued the art with more attention to its finer aspects. After the initiation, the children could go on with their other interests without having to worry about lessons. Then, usually around the age of 15 to 18, the prospective good dancers learned that their successes in hunting and fishing went together with their peers' desires that they do as well in the dance. This mode of teaching the young leaves the individual to make choices.

Now, with the young moving to other areas, the disruption of family life, and western influence, the original Eskimo dance has not survived well. Some form of it is done as a tourist attraction. Nevertheless, the Eskimo dance continues to exist. I believe a revival of this art is imminent. From all the above, it should be clear that the arts of dancing and singing, in Eskimo culture, was a most important part of the culture, as well as of the social life.

To burst the bubble of still another misconception, Eskimo children were not carried in the hood of the mother's parka. If this were done, the mother would always have an uncomfortable feeling about the throat. Infants were carried by slipping them behind the mother's back, the baby's head being outside of the hood. In Wales, I remember there was a great demand for wide leather belts, the kind I assume were worn by fat cowboys. They were used for holding the baby in place while being carried. This was done by having the child's legs resting on the belt, under the parka, and fastening the buckle atop the breasts.

One of the earlier works done on the Eskimo was by Hubert Howe Bancroft (Volume I, *The Native Races*). Printed in 1883, it is a curious collection of impressions, thoughts, facts, and imaginative exaggerations. About the Eskimo, at one point he states:

> "The Russians compelled the natives of the Aleutian Islands to hunt sea-animals. The filthy raw-flesh-eating Eskimos, having nothing wherewith to tempt the cupidity of the superior race, retain their primitive purity."

Bancroft describes the Eskimos as "Hyperboreans," which, according to Webster, is derived from Greek mythology, meaning "One of a people beyond the north wind in a region of perpetual sunshine." As an adjective it means "of or in the far north; hence, cold."

Other areas which are considered by my parents as *Eh sah ne* are involved with certain old-time practices, such as Shamanism, tattooing, and other matters of ancient custom. Their attitude is understandable. Such things no longer belong in their way of life at Nome. They are striving mightily to adjust to another culture, a foreign culture, in which the struggle for mere existence is so much more difficult than it was in the old days, so much less satisfying. Who can blame them. Still, the ancient memory persists, and the old ways remain in the subconscious, known and loved, and even still feared.

Before the advent of Christian ideology in Northwest Alaska, the Eskimo's spiritual life dealt with things necessarily within the realm of nature, as a combination of forces and organic-inorganic matter. These beliefs are opposed to the idea of some personalized Savior coming from some far-away place of origin, bringing The Word. The Eskimo was living within his environment as well as he could. His tools, customs, ideas of personal and family well-being all show how well he adapted to the conditions of life. He met these conditions with tolerance and ingenuity. Our religious beliefs and practices were so ancient in their origins that the natives themselves could not explain them. Even in modern times, when I was a child at Wales, they could not fully explain the methods used by the Shamans or "Angakoks" for exercising their supernatural powers. Here, the qualities of both tolerance and ingenuity came to be the main factors of such a religious practice as Shamanism. From the point of view of a man who has been subjected to many and varied types of beliefs, I believe that Christian denominations are today beginning to question their old ways. There is developing a need to respect all religions, a need to unify all in one great regard for something better, something higher, something nobler than we are now.

I cannot see why Shamanism could not also be modernized and "merged" into the life of the modern Eskimo. Man travels fast, both spiritually and physically, in this age. The best of all cultures ought to be preserved, for the preservation of Man himself. It is so with religion as well. I ask myself: Have the well-meaning Christian churches in Alaska, Canada, and Greenland already

THE BIRD HUNTER

erased all vestiges of some spiritual power which could have been their tool in living with and "serving" the natives? Is it too late?

The custom of tattooing is gone, among the Eskimos of Alaska. The old woman who lived with us at Wales until about 1946 had tattoos on her chin. This consisted of about five or six vertical lines which started from the base of the lower lip and ended on the most prominent part of the chin. She put an "instructional" tattoo on my older sister's chin. It was quite small and is today practically unnoticeable. The tattoo was done by rubbing a piece of reindeer sinew with soot, and then passing a needle through the epidermis. Even in that day, the practice of tattooing had disappeared. It was gone in my mother's generation. She herself has no tattoo. I have never seen a male Eskimo with a labret (lip plug), so that this custom must have died even earlier than the practice of tattooing. Such customs as tattooing, the use of labrets, and others, were associated with the beliefs of the people, and observance of certain customs. The use of such devices brings up the whole question as to what is beauty? What is beautiful?

Americans, provincial as they are, and also generally the people of the western world, see none other than themselves as the epitome of all that is best, all that is holiest, and all that is most beautiful. Closer contact with the rest of the people of this earth would show entirely different standards of beauty. It is all in the eye of the beholder, the beholder being himself the result of his ancient heritage, his beliefs, and his workable lifeways.

As a modern Eskimo man, with a family of my own, I reject *Eh Sah Ne,* and strive to understand all peoples, to respect all religions, to think of nothing as "strange," and to practice the art of loving and living well with my neighbors of the world.

10

The Hunter

It is pitch dark outdoors. There is not a sound except for a slight humming noise coming from the wood stove. The wood burned down to its grey and white ashes seven hours ago, after the stove was charged for the last time before the family turned in for the night. Among the ashes are bleached dried bones from the evening meal. The humming noise emanating from the stove is the wind, picked up by the guy wires of the stovepipe. It wheezes down the eight feet of pipe and the echo chamber formed by the combustion area. The ash box sends the sound of the wind to the ears of the man just awaking. It is cold. The eyes open and close without determining the difference between sight and darkness. In a normal tone of voice, the man calls, "Helen."

A rustle of bedding and a creak of bedsprings. Now he hears the ticking of the clock, rises and goes to the stove as he has always done. He feels for the matches on the stove shelf. Finding them, he lights the kerosene lantern while his wife rises and puts on her parka over her slip. She pushes back her hair in the dim light of the lantern, slips on a pair of mukluks, and shuffles over to the camp stove. Joe and Cora are still in bed, but Joe starts to wake to the noise of the camp stove being pumped with air. Swish, swish, swish, SQUEAK! Swish, swish, swish, SQUEAK! Squeak, swish, swish. Rattle, rattle — the camp stove's air pump is closing. Another match is struck and the flame slowly starts its hissing and fills the small room with a small roar.

There is more rattling of pots and pans. The ice in the water barrel is broken. Water is poured and the coffee pot is placed on the camp stove. The man goes to the bedside and gathers his clothes. He puts on a pair of black Levi's and a couple of pairs of mismatched wool socks. A heavy wool shirt is donned over his wool longjohns. Then he goes to the wood stove and makes some wood shavings with his hunting knife. He places the kindling in the stove. He takes a small piece of wood and holds it over the flame of the camp stove, transfers the flame to the kindling. He takes the bigger pieces and builds up the fire. It will continue to burn all day. He reaches for the knee length hunting mukluks behind the stove and checks to see if the grass insoles are dry and sufficient for his workday.

By this time the coffee is boiling and the wife opens a round package of rolled oats and begins to prepare breakfast for the family. Joe, still in bed, takes in the sounds of the morning, waiting for the heat to reach his corner of the room where he sleeps on a wooden bunk bed atop another one where Cora sleeps. This wooden bunk bed, about four feet wide by five feet long, had slept five before Cora and him, three above and two below. This was before their oldest sister and their two older brothers went away to a boarding school. The room is about ten by twelve. The smell of "mussak" (mush or cereal), coffee, and sourdough pancakes swirls over to his corner and his mother does not have to coax him too much. He jumps down and walks sleepily over to the corner by the door to relieve himself. He does this into a Sears chamber pot, white enameled.

Cora gets up and does the same. She says she doesn't feel too well and her mother asks the usual questions, "Where does it hurt?"

"Here."

Her head is felt for temperature. She is given a glass of half evaporated milk and water, and a motherly, "You'll be better soon. We'll have Aukoruk (grandmother) look at you." Aukoruk and the words village midwife, sage, and wise old woman who takes care of upset stomachs, are synonymous.

There are few words at the breakfast table. The table is a piece of plywood about four feet square, with an elevated bottom frame of about two inches. It is cleaned and put aside after the meals. Now it is set down in the center of the room. The hot pot of mush is placed on it. The sugar bowl is identical with the mush bowls. They are the thick white ceramic type, very utilitarian, with a rounded top edge. The oleo and its yellowing powder are mixed and placed on an enameled plate, white with a dark blue edge. Joe is also given a glass of milk but it is not the special mixture of half and half given to Cora. It is the usual seven-eighths water and an eighth evaporated milk.

It is now six-thirty, mid-February, and the dawn's light is still two and a half hours away. The man packs his hunting bag, a sealskin affair made of one whole small seal which has been meticulously skinned, tanned, bleached and sewn with a foot and a half slit on top. A thicker hide serves as the carrying strap. He fills his pint thermos with coffee and milk and lots of sugar. Puts in a couple of pieces of dried seal meat, a few dried tom cod and some pilot bread. He then automatically checks the contents which are already inside the bag: a long length of seal raw-hide rope. A seal retrieving hook which looks like a big four-hook fish-hook with body of wood shaped like a light bulb. He checks the points which are protected with carefully carved wooden plugs tied to the body with reindeer sinew. Two boxes of 25-35 ammunition. A razorsharp hunting knife in a walrus hide sheath. A pair of well worn seven-power binoculars with the black coating worn off, showing the whitish-grey metal and a piece of cotton twine to secure the adjustment knob and to provide a makeshift carrying strap. Extra pairs of socks and a heavy pair of wolfskin mittens. A seal drag harness. Spare snaps for the dog harnesses. Matches, and sewing kit in a bandaid metal box. Nothing else, just the bare necessities. He remembers when, at one time, there was the need to take along a good luck charm carved out of ivory so that the animal spirits would not be offended.

Everything is in order. The room, small as it is, now feels warmer, and he does not want to get too used to the comfortable warmth. He quickens his preparations for the hunt by putting on his first object of concern, the mukluks. He knows that the hands and feet are the most vulnerable and most needed for his job. The skin boots are made of the choicest materials available and are sewn with the greatest care and utmost utilization of skin-sewing skill the wife has learned. He has already pulled the very important sealskin pants over his Levis. These are not altogether Eskimo design, since the very top part is comprised of the upper remnants of an older pair of denim pants, making use of the belt loops and pockets. Not to mention the fly. The sealskins are sewn with the fur side out to complete the warmest pair of pants made. The mukluks are made of pliable defurred seal uppers and tough bearded seal soles. The tie thongs around the ankles are fastened carefully so that, in an emergency, they can be untied quickly, but tied securely so that they do not accidently untie. The boot upper is hemmed by a felt edge through which a cotton string rope passes. This too is tied in a manner which will enable the wearer to untie easily.

He puts on his squirrel skin parka topped with a heavy white parka cover and says goodbye to his wife, "I plan to be up near the vicinity of the light station. Maybe I'll be able to catch a good seal out at the seal net. Expect me back before nightfall."

"Yes, remember the brown youngster was limping yesterday."

He grabs a pair of jersey gloves and his hat from the nail by the door and leaves by going through the first storage room, then through the front storage room, out to the snow tunnel to which he annually fixes two by four joists, to hold the weight of the overhead snow. His house is peculiarly situated, so that a giant snow drift blows over his home from behind and the snow tunnel runs a good fifteen feet from the front door, up snow steps to the outside. He doesn't mind the extra work involved, since the snow is a very good insulator and this saves on driftwood for the stove. It is still fairly dark outdoors, but when he looks toward Cape Prince of Wales, it is outlined by a dim bluish light. The stars are still visible. He checks for signs of good or bad weather by studying the cloud formations. It looks normal, and he walks over to the dog shed. One of the dogs wakes up and looks intently at the man, recognizes him, yawns loudly, and stretches. The other dogs are immediately awake. The dog shed is a simple structure made of found lumber. It is about fifteen by ten and the inside is broken up into compartments where the dogs are separated by partitions. Maybe it's better to call it a dog barn. It smells. The younger dogs get excited and make a commotion while the older dogs know what is going on.

He goes over to the dog sled. It is turned over, so he grabs the runner and shakes it to free it from the night's snow drifts, and he turns it roughly again to shake some more snow off. The dog sled looks as if it would not be able to take so much rough handling. It is built to be as light as it looks, but like the skin boat, it is made of strong wood and the joints are lashed together with rawhide rope. He goes back to the front storeroom and gets the sled bag and the trace. He fastens the bag to the rear part of the sled below the hand rail. It contains a couple of fishing lines wound on their jigger handles, more rope, his harpoon head and some repair material for his seal net. He sets the trace on the snow in front of the sled, checking the snaps and individual traces spliced to the main trace; he also snaps together the harnesses to the lines. He wonders if he should take along the young limping dog. "He may have stepped on something sharp and needs the time to recuperate . . . I'll check him out and see how he does today", he thinks to himself, "He needs the experience if he is going to earn his living."

He knows that he needs all of the energy which the dogs furnish for his work day. This relies on carefully made decisions which will enable the dogs to continue to be healthy and alert. He knows that his forefathers did not have the modern steel runners, the rope trace, the steel brake, the web harness, and the rifle. He is vaguely aware of the times when the runners were prepared with seal blubber frozen on the wood. When the traces were made of the all-important rawhide rope, which took a long time to make, but a short while for the dogs to chew up and eat. When preparations for the hunt took so much longer, and the short daylight of the winters meant so much in order to find game and procure them without a rifle. When the dogs were more susceptible to internal disease like worms and distemper.

"Yes, this is so much easier. If only it was possible that I could continue school", he muses. "Maybe there are other careers such as prospecting or schoolteaching which are even easier than this. But one has to eat; to raise a family and provide them with food. . . . "

He goes back and gets the rifle, and on second thought brings along a set of dog boots which he has recently made out of canvas. He goes and gets the lead dog. Snaps him in place. Then the rear two. Then the front two, the young brown one as one of them. He wants the younger ones in front to see if they have possibilities of becoming future leaders. Four more are harnessed and by now they are all showing excitement and can be heard from inside the house. He scolds a couple for being so frisky, lest they tangle the lines. He piles his load on the sled and ties them up to the long slats and at last picks up the anchor hook. The lead dog stays in place until the man gives his order, "MUSS!"

The leader leaps forward, mainly to obey, but also to keep from being run over by the eager team. The man uses his foot brake to keep control since he has a light load. He has to keep balancing the sled by alternately jumping from one runner to the other. The front of the sled bounces up and down as it passes every little wave of snow drift.

"GEE!" The lead dog, perhaps wondering where the master wants to go today, takes longer to obey. "ZEE! GEEH!", the man shouts while pushing his foot brake down harder. This brake is a long board about four inches wide, tied to the front lateral and running underneath the sled to the rear, where it is held up by a long loose spring. The braking action is done by means of a metal plate which looks like large saw teeth attached to the end of the board. The leader understands, and swings to the right, heading to the trail below the village which goes to a main trail leading North along the smooth beach. It is not a straight line, because of such obstacles as huge snow drifts and ice blocks which during the fall were pushed up near the shore line by tides and currents. But the leader knows now, through many previous trips, where he is to go. The other dogs know that all they have to do is to follow him.

It takes about an hour to get to the landmark, the light station which is about ten miles up the coast. The light station is a battery-operated light encased in a small wooden structure atop a knoll. It is now dead, and will not operate until the spring coast guard boat comes to recharge it. Not many ships will use it, but there is one evidence of its need not far away: the front section of some long forgotten whaling ship, now buried under the ice and snow, but starkly visible in the summertime. A reminder to all who have the temerity to frequent the stormy waters of the Bering Strait. For some time now the dogs have found their own gait and the man has no need to calm them down. He frequently runs beside the sled to exercise and keep warm. "Hah!" The lead dog turns left and out from the main trail, which continues all the way up to another village, Shishmaref, 70 miles from Wales. The lesser trail is used by a number of Wales men who then make their own trails to their hunting grounds. This trail is less smooth. Some places have to be traveled with the combined effort of the man and his dogs, so that the sled is not pulled too far to the left or right where it might be dropped into a chasm formed by huge pressure ridges, or wedged into deceptive smaller ice formations. Then there are some places where early snows, salt water leakage, and ice movements of the freezeup in the last stages of Fall have caused the present surface snow to form very thin ice underneath, with a lot of insulating snow between. These are usually recognized by the experienced hunter; and they do not occur often. But even experienced hunters make mistakes now and then.

Due now to more difficult travel, the man stops for a rest. He puts on his sunglasses, for the sun from the East is now shining very brightly upon the snow. The dogs rest, their mouths open, tongues out, and vapor emitting from them. Some move around to smell the trail as if they were curious to know if other dogs had recently traveled through this area. The young brown has lost his limp considerably, but he sits on the snow quietly.

"Muss' Ghee Uttah!" (Go! Let us at it again!) He talks the dogs up. They start the pulling, while the man lifts up on the sled rail to loosen the runners. He has to continually use the brake to offset the sliding on the downhill slopes of the rugged trail, and to push uphill on the next rise.

The only sounds the man hears now are his own breathing which is coming in and out hard; the different noises the sled runners make on different types of snow surfaces; the creaking of the whole sled as it is moved sideways and forward; at times the sound of the dogs' foot pads on hard snow, and the scraping of the brake whenever it is applied.

They finally reach the seal net place and the man throws down the snow anchor, a big iron hook tied to the trace so that the sled does not take the stress on its slender stanchions. The seal net area is marked with a long pole, but the man knows its whereabouts by the ice formations. This is a remarkable aspect of the seal hunter, to be so familiar with a place out on the ice, because even in the midst of so many different piles of snow and ice, it always seems to the non-hunter, to be a surrounding made up of the same jumble, no matter where it is on the ice.

The man goes to the pole, a rope is tied to it. The rope runs down to the ice and disappears in the snow, which has drifted to the blow hole area. He takes hold of the rope and follows it to the hole, which has now frozen, with a layer of ice a couple of inches thick. He unties his "touk", a long handled ice chisel, from the sled, and breaks apart the ice to free the rope. In a few minutes he has made a big enough hole to pull up on the rope and to check the net. This is a seal hide net tied together much like a big salmon gill net. Its squares are about four by four so that any seal looking for the blow hole will get caught and drown, because of its inability to use its claws to dig upwards on the bottom side of the ice. He finds it empty, so he lowers it again. He hopes that the hole he has just chopped will entice a seal to try using it, but he knows that the seals are wary animals and he should remain away for a while. He looks outward to sea, where there is still a couple of miles to some leads (open water) and readies the team for the trek to the nearest lead. This trail is even less used, so he has to compromise between his desire to go as fast as possible, and wanting to conserve his team for the trip back. It is always tough going on the ice, even when it looks very smooth from afar. Trying to keep the sled upright, keeping it from slamming the rears of the closest dogs on the downgrades, giving the leader strict commands while making tight maneuvers, makes the man breathe hard, his lungs refusing to take in so much cold air at once. He grabs the snow anchor while on an upgrade, and a good thing he did! He steps off from the trail about a foot, and his whole right side drops into soft snow. In the same instant he throws the anchor down, as his team keeps going.

He is now lying face down on the snow, and his whole right leg is straight down, resting on nothing firm. He sees the dogs stop abruptly. The leader looks back to see what the trouble is. Feeling a little foolish, the man takes about two minutes to free himself. It is difficult to get off the snow when there are no real hand holds or braces. He rocks back and forth to enlarge the cavity made by his leg. Then he has to pull straight out with his foot stretched out. Having thrown the snow anchor, he has evaded the embarrassing situation of a hunter losing his team. Not a few young hunters in Wales have to walk all the way home because of any number of precautionary measures not taken. The lessons are well learned, after a few mishaps. Inexperienced hunters do not have the confidence of a team of dogs who have been trained by the more experienced master, so the empty team will nearly always return home if the sled has managed to remain upright.

He cusses . . . "Goddam!" mainly in laughter at himself for having made a dumb move. The "Goddam" he rarely uses except when very angry, and then it is said in the meanest manner his children have ever heard. To "swayk-tuk" or swear is something which he and the villagers have learned from the few "outsiders" who have frequented Wales, but rarely. So it is more of a figure of speech than actually "taking in vain the name of God". But the children have learned differently from teachers, Moms, and Church, so they cringe when and if someone lets go.

He reaches the lead without further accidents. He looks back at the land, and the far hills are plainly visible. An indication that there are no undue winds which may imperil his return trip. There are no threatening clouds on the hilltops. He scans the water to look for seals. None. He climbs a jutting ice clump which rises some twenty feet. Looks around with his binoculars. He sees a seal resting on the ice about a half mile away. But he decides to wait for one from the lead's edge. He sits down and waits.

Waiting out on the ice is something that no man can do without feeling some comprehension of his place as man, his environment, and the forces of the air, the water, and his own make-up. It all swirls around in a sort of subconscious thought; his conscious thought is full of the need to provide for oneself and others.

"Not too long ago, other men sat here and thought of the same things," he ponders, "It might not have been the exact same place, but it was surely the same time of the year.

"As sure as I am here, one of them might have had exactly the same line of thought. He was less fortunate in that he did not have the rifle. He was less fortunate in that he believed that the seal needed appeasement before being caught. His chances of catching a seal were perhaps fifty times as slim as my chances. No. It wasn't the same line of thought. It was different in those days. I'm waiting here thinking I will soon be visited by a seal and I will be able to sit very still so that he will not see me sitting here. He waited here because he felt there was some inhuman sort of communications with the Lady Spirit of the Sea who had the power to offer him a chance. I'm waiting because there is a possibility of a sea mammal coming up for air here.

"I don't know. Who knows? He had children and they had children and it comes to *now*. Here I am. Here we are. Me, the same waters which freeze to the same types of ice and snow, the same types of dogs, the same types of seals. But my family is different. They could have more of a chance. I mean my children and their children can have more. A chance not to sit here and freeze the butt. A chance to aim at more profitable things. No, we are not different; he wanted to survive. So do I."

He lines the sights of his rifle on an imaginary seal about fifty yards away. Moves it to a floating bit of ice.

"If you were a seal, how much of a chance would I have if I were to plant my feet firmly on the snow, aim very carefully, become very still, hardly breathing. And . . . and a slow pull of the trigger . . ." He checks himself on the pulling of the trigger but continues to daydream, "In a split second there would be a loud noise, my ears would feel strangely pushed back . . . my ears starting to ring, a faint chunk as the bullet hits the skull.

"I would see the bits of brain fly before I hear the dull noise. I would breathe again. I would rejoice. I would be exalted. Run to the sled and grab the seal hoo . . ."

A seal emerges from the blue-grey waters a little to the left of the place where he has kept his sights. It takes him a second to wake from his daydream and his peripheral vision causes his eyes to swing leftward only to see the seal bobbing upward to his neck base before quickly dropping out of sight. There is a small ripple left on the spot where he is now aiming.

The hunter is wary and scans the water with added attention for the next breeching of the seal head. On a clear day the seal head appears smaller than on a cloudy day. He doesn't quite know how large the seal is, because he got only a glimpse. If it is a large one, it will be able to hold its breath longer and may be on its way to another lead. Or it may be a large one and is curious enough to take another look at the strange, man-animal on the ice.

An average seal can stay under for ten to twenty minutes. It seems like an hour when one is expecting it to reappear. No drug trip this, just the mind working extra hard after so much physical exertion. And it is not what the hunter enjoys, as some writers on the Eskimo would have it. Some say that the Eskimo likes to feel coldness and its effects on mind and body. It is nerve wracking to be so much at the mercy of almighty weather and chance. What a hunter enjoys is the past experience of having had the opportunity to secure food and clothing. He remembers with pleasure that it was at such a time and such a place. The very source of investing the mind and the tools, the dogs, the sled, the weapon and physical fitness. Quite an investment, since many a hunter has had the misfortune of dying out on the ice, to leave wife and children in the care of other hunters . . .

"When the seal shows up, I must try hard to control my shivering. I have lived thus far, and I must continue living, so that no great interruption will upset my family and their well-being."

Some flashes of incidents that have nearly caused a broken family come to his mind. Twice buried under avalanches. Twice broken through thin ice, once with the dogs. Once so tired from walking all day keeping track of the reindeer herd, that it was all he could do not to give up, without food and water. Quite a few times, with the boat crew caught between stormy seas and crunching ice floes. A few times, when angry walrus herds tried to ram the skin boat. About four times, when he saw his part of the shore ice starting to move out to sea, once with his oldest son, Ron, and another great hunter and son threatened by this ever present danger. Another time when his trap was holding a very much alive wolverine, after he thought he had finished it off.

The seal pops up at about the same place. He squeezes off a shot. The loud report and all of what he had imagined earlier happens, but *he misses*. Instead of the "Chunk", he hears a "Splat" as the bullet strikes the water a little to the left. The wind is blowing from the right and a gust must have made him miss. He decides to wait some more.

It is now close to ten o'clock and he is starting to feel hungry. In the old days, a hunter did not eat until he had caught something. But he is hungry, and he goes to the hunting bag and takes a bite of dried seal meat. He returns to his waiting place.

"If I were to be paid for doing this, how much would I be worth?" He asks nobody in particular, "How much can a person get to put on all the work that I do?"

"It's nothing if anything happens to me. Chances are that if anything happens to me that Ron, Skip, and Joe would have to ask this sort of question with the same big question mark. If Iwere to go to Nome . . . if I were to go there . . . What sort of a job could I find there? I know something of mining and something of prospecting now . . . I would be able to work and be at a place where the younger boys can go to high school and maybe learn what I did not learn. Ah! Dreamer! I've grown to this! Miss a close seal, and my mind wanders to foolish thoughts."

He gets up to relieve himself. In a world of white, blues and greys, the odd yellow stream bores its own dark little well to forever stain that bit of ice until it melts someplace, some time.

Around eleven-thirty, he decides that he had better head back to the net area, so that he can check the net once more before returning home. He reloads the sled. "Gee! Gee!" he cries with an almost angry voice. Angry at his misfortune and the thought of having had a lapse of self-confidence as to his abilities . . . and at a time calling for strict attention to his work. The dogs wheel to the right, as he holds the rear of the sled in place, pivoting the whole around. He looks for any stragglers among the rearward dogs. He spots one who is too eager, and threatens to cross up over his main trace, and cries to him, "Tippy! Tippy! Stay! Stay!"

When he reaches the seal net, he finds the line taut. This lifts up his spirits and he runs to the line. He pulls on it to make certain. Indeed the weight has become slightly heavier. He cleans up the hole, and a short time is spent in pulling up the net, which gets heavier and heavier and the now frozen seal looms into view through the dark water. His hands feel numb and cold, but he takes his knife and cuts a slit from the lip to the eye, passing the end of his seal-pull through the slit, and then he loops the open end over the snout. He pulls, with tremendous effort, to "land" the animal. He slips the net off, and checks it for damage. Two squares are in need of repair, so he first reaches inside his shirt under his arms, to warm his brown and weathered hands, before starting this needed additional work. If one had x-ray vision and could see those hands next to the body, it would seem they belonged to another person, his body is so surprisingly white in contrast to his hands. Now he feels the peculiar and uncomfortable sensation of "burning" in his hands. This means the return of blood circulation. It takes him fifteen minutes to repair the net and re-set it. He takes another fifteen minutes to load the seal and tie it down. Finally he sits down for lunch. The hot coffee tastes bitter sweet. It warms his whole body and he has a sense of well-being. In the cold, clean air, he fairly glows as he bites into the rest of the dried meat, the taste buds unhampered by smells from other sources. Even the plain pilot bread exudes its own full flavor, as he washes it down with the coffee.

Now he finishes his lunch and goes to the young dog, who seems to be doing well but still favors his right front leg. He holds up the paw and takes another look between the pads. It is hard to tell, since the husky grows fur between them, and the grooves are deep. He decides to put a dog boot on him. This is done, and again he sets out to go back through the jumble of ice and snow. Since he has added about eighty pounds of spotted seal, the ups and downs of the trail are a little easier for him to control, except for the side slanting ones. This makes him work twice as hard, to keep the sled from sliding sideways to soft snow or hard ice. The dogs don't noticeably feel the difference, since they can haul many times more weight before they show signs of balking. The heavier loads are pulled on the more sluggish sledge, with runners a couple of inches wider than the hunting sled, and the height of the sledge runners average six or seven inches.

As Willie Senungetuk reaches the smoother going of the secondary trail leading inland, he is again struck by thoughts which earlier had floated around in his mind, and once again he muses:

"Here I am, my arms and legs are still intact and I could use them to work with . . . to be employed by someone . . . someone like Mr. Christensen, or Mr. Crane . . . I would be able to return home every evening without worrying about dogs or the weather. It won't be so hard, after I have learned all about the job. That would be the only tough time . . . my children will adapt easily . . . it is only I who will have a problem. Helen will be able to visit her friends in Nome, and they will help us out. Also, my brother should be able to help me start there. I have saved up a good part of my pay from Buck Creek Tin Mining. That two summers' work did me good . . . and there's the gold mining in Nome . . ."

The sun has now started its westward dive, and the afternoon westerly wind has begun to sweep the surface of the ice, making odd ridges on the trail. The footprints and sled with parallel tracks take on the form of photographic negatives when viewed from above. If one keeps track of the windy and calm days, he could tell just when the tracks were made, by the size of the small humps. They are probably caused by the minute elevations made by the pressure of the feet and sled runners, as well as the depressions which the surface winds ride over, causing a mini-turbulence. Like an airfoil. When they freeze overnight, they become larger obstructions, and build up to inverted monster-sized prints. These make the trail bumpy and easy to follow, even with the phenomena of the snake-like movements of the powdery snow being transported many surface miles.

His glasses are now more of a hindrance than an aid against the bright slanting rays of the sun, which intensify the movement of the blowing snow. The metal temples of his glasses are like two ice rods pressing against his skin, and the lens fogs up the instant his vaporous breath hits it. He slips the glasses off, and shoves them into his large stomach pocket. Squinting, he wonders if the manufactured sunglasses are so much better than the goggles invented by his ancestors.

He runs for quite a distance beside the sled, to build up his circulation, his one hand on the rail, then jumps back on the foot rest when he feels there is enough balance between circulation and body perspiration. Since he does not have a lot of body hair, his first indication of perspiration is from his feet and hands. Through years of all this exercise-work, the soles of his feet are covered with thick callouses, which have extended to the upper part of the little toe. These he has to shave off periodically, because his little toe-nails also have a tendency to grow with the callouses. This is the only problem in wearing hunting mukluks, with the hard sewn edge on the joint between uppers and soles.

Now halfway home, the dogs instinctively speed up, and their rhythmic movement, a familiar sight, quickens the man's spirits. He takes another long jog, feeling he will be home soon, safe. The wind is picking up, and the swirling motion changes to an eerie downward movement which appears to be quite still, moving very slowly and yet very fast at intervals, depending upon how close or how near you looked. It fades the legs of the front dogs, so that they look as if they were legless forms undulating amid the heavens. Screech! One of the steel runners passes over a rock, or sand, which has been bared by the uplift of last Fall's ice formation and the winds. Generations earlier he would have had to stop and repair a runner coat by urinating on it for a fast repair, or stop and make a preparation of seal blubber mend.

The last half mile or so is short, due to the increasing speed of the dogs, racing to be home to rest. He rides the front rails, and they climb the rise to the village while he shifts his weight almost sportingly.

The darkening hours are spent tying back the dogs to their stations, and putting away the gear. The seal is stored in the front storage room, and the frozen state it is in keeps the "yard," snow steps, and shed clean.

The two children are sent out to feed the dogs. They use a flashlight, and the young girl is very cautious while the big brave brother reaches quickly for the feed pots, large coffee cans, quartered five gallon containers, discarded pots and pans, and even an old pan roaster . . . all used as containers. They fill these up with the left-over bones and soups which the family has saved up to make "Ahleeyuk" or "slop," a mixture of grains and left-overs, and the poorer quality of dried meats. The dogs are ravenously hungry, and the noise of their strong jaws breaking up the bones are more reason for the children not to get too close. In the smallish barn, dark and cold and smelly, there is a mixture of awe and the desire to get out of there as soon as possible for the younger, while the older one dispenses orders, "Here, take this to Tippy. This one to the end dog." He is earnestly and secretly proud to be part of the help in getting the seal home. The job done, they race each other in getting back to the house.

Once inside, they hear the father say, ". . . had some thought about it today. Well, I have been thinking on and off about it. I have made up my mind. We have a good family . . . I do all right hunting here . . . but to buy rifles, clothing, sugar, coffee, milk, tea and other things, it takes working for wages. I've saved up about four hundred and eighty dollars, working at the tin mines. I have enough for transportation to Nome, for the family. I'll sell the house and hunting equipment. The dogs . . . some I'll give away and some I can sell. Right now, I don't owe anyone here and the money I get from the house, the boat, the dogs, the sleds, and my shotgun . . . we can use it to live on in Nome while I look for a job. I'll write to Nick tomorrow and see if he can find a place for us to sleep."

The year was 1950.

THE "WOLF KILLER"

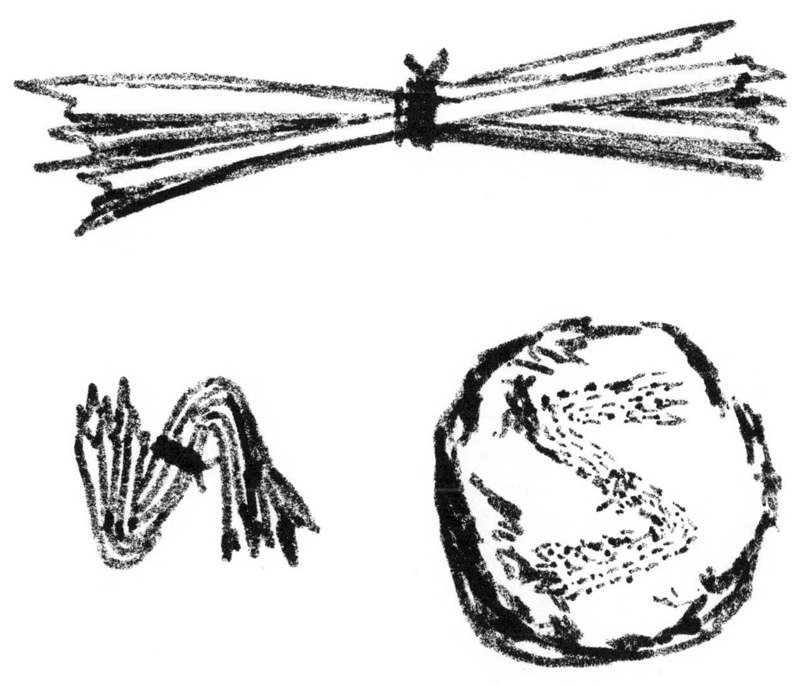

Made of baleen. A bunch of sharp, pointed strips (top), were bent (left center) and frozen inside a ball of seal blubber (right center). Strips are approximately a foot long. Used before introduction of steel traps.

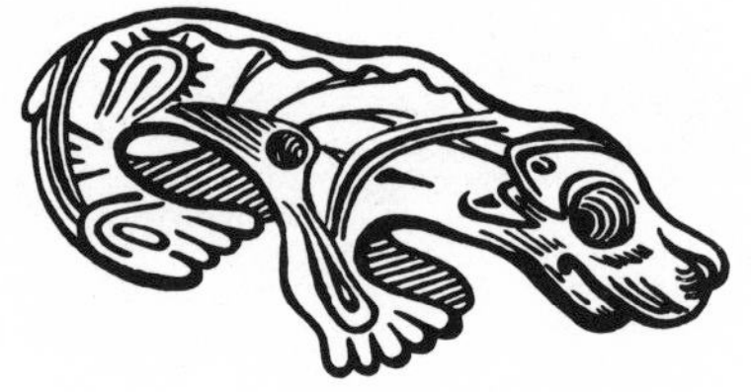

11

To Nome with Deep Regret

Consider the immensity of the choice that Willie Senungetuk found it necessary to make in 1950. He had grown up in his own little area of the world. But this small spot was part of an ancient land base, thousands of years old. The early Eskimos had knowledge of the vastness of their land, which they occupied and cared for with love and devotion, with tremendous respect for its natural integrity. Willie inherited this tradition. It was part of his heart and mind. His very soul was tied to it. A move to Nome would deprive him of the sense of belonging and *owning* a great and marvelous land. In Nome, one *buys* land today. No individual Eskimo is so rich that he can afford to buy a parcel of land. If he is actually to own land, he will measure it by the white man's standards. So many acres . . . so many dollars. So many feet, by actual present-day measurement. The early Eskimo had exceptional and skillful intertribal communication. He traveled extensively on foot, by skin boat or dog sled. Knowledge of the geography and food sources was a normal part of the lives of villagers, hundreds and sometimes thousands of miles apart.

In a city like Nome, one travels by plane, or by car. This takes money. Thus is cut off the ancient knowledge of the people . . . the knowledge of themselves, the knowledge of their tribesmen, and their knowledge of the land. It is a strange and forbidding fact, that *communication* is the greatest need among the people today. We Eskimos, whom historical research has described as "primitive, uncivilized, technologically backward," knew more about one another before European technological influence wrested our land from us, than we do today, when the most modern and sophisticated methods of travel known to man, are available but beyond our reach.

And so Willie was confronted by this choice: To remain in his Wales ancestral village and let the Bureau of Indian Affairs take care of the education of all his children. Or, to move to Nome and undertake the independent role of provider, husband, father of grade school children, taxpayer, home-owner, good neighbor. All this loomed on the horizon of his questioning mind. He knew that his children must be prepared for a different world than he had known. He was fully aware of the need for their education. But, he thought, how much training did *he* have for living in Nome? Such problems as knowledge of the English language, a foreign tongue, would be his to solve. Problems such as being capable of working in a technological system entirely different from his own. Then too, in the village of Wales he was secure. No matter how difficult it is to live there, many Eskimos still treasure the security of their own village, even when they know there are better opportunities for their children elsewhere. Village life in Wales did not prepare one for life in the world at large. Willie himself had been given no opportunities for such preparation.

Hence, Willie Senungetuk turned over and over in his mind this choice. And as he thought, the situation of Wales village occupied him in making a judgment which in his own mind would be best for his family. During the past twenty years, Wales has experienced few occasions when new, outside economy penetrated its autonomous fabric of self-ruling, self-sustaining economy. There were such Eskimo people as "well-to-do," and "not-as-well-to-do." Such terms, however, questionable as they are in describing Eskimo society, might better have been applied to families instead of to individuals. Wales villagers depended for their livelihood upon their ability to conquer the natural economy, to live within it. The whole village would be forced to go a little hungry if some segment of a hunting season proved unproductive, or not productive enough to feed the village families as a whole. Even today, in a place like Nome, those who remember their lives in villages like Wales will sacrifice their "riches," their possessions if they have any, their importance, and their whole selves, in order to see that their families eat and continue to eat. This is not because they deem themselves as individual persons unimportant, but because among the villages providers must provide.

Economic status depended not on monetary standards. It was rather that the "well-to-do" had more elaborate hunting gear, larger houses; quite often they had larger families, more dogs for the dog sled, better shelters for the dogs. And the master of the house was generally known to possess keener senses and abilities in hunting. That is, he knew when to be cautious and when to be more carefree in his hunting style, among other things. During the hungry times, the more well-to-do, who naturally had more storage space for food, had less reason to be concerned about their family's needs. The master of such a household became the leader in hunts, and this required unusual knowledge, skill, and bravery.

When I was about six years old, my father was beginning to add to his hunting gear. Through his efforts to be a provider to the best of his ability, he managed to gain employment from various sources, at odd times and for sporadic durations. Those were the days when he worked for a dollar a day, or, during good working conditions, for five dollars a day. In the Wales village society, having no monetary standards, and more especially during those years of the 1940's, payment for goods or services meant that the individual received a certificate, good for exchange for items which were not available by capturing or gathering. The fact that a huge government existed in Washington, just recovering from an economic depression; that this government was about to involve itself with other foreign governments in a war, and that the dollar represented some faraway bank system, meant very little to Wales society. It was not directly affected. For Willie Senungetuk, it meant he must apply what he had learned in the Bureau of Indian Affairs school at Wales. This training gave him some small degree of dollars and cents knowledge. It was all he was able to comprehend at this seventh grade level, and nothing was done to help him learn skills, trades, or business methods. Seventh grade arithmetic during his time taught basic elementary addition and subtraction, and the multiplication table. It went not much further than the one-thousands. Ancient Eskimo society in Wales had no need to deal with numbers larger than a few hundreds. In fact, in a good spring hunting season, the share of collective hunting for each member of a hunting party did not exceed fifty for the number of small game such as ducks or fish. It was enough.

With this degree of arithmetical knowledge, and a basic though inadequate understanding of reading and writing, Willie found he had some capacity for dealing with the fairly new influx of outside opportunities. By the time he had his own family to care for, he could use this capacity to its fullest extent. Unfortunately, his abilities were not enough to contend with those who make payment for work or services. As a further point, those who pay are themselves unlearned about Willie's standards, which deal with human values, the rewards of the earth going directly to the recipients through hard work, highly specialized native technological knowledge, and energy. Imagine the overall outcome of such early dealings with a strange and foreign culture!

Those were Willie's thoughts and his memories, as churned up through his personal experience. In retrospect, my own memories are blended with experiences in Nome, and what I have thought and pondered upon over and over since those days of choice and change.

A girl playmate in Wales who had visited Nome with her family and with whom I talked and played, with a freedom later lost, had become aware of Nome, the supercity, through her own eyes.

"In Nome, the bushes which bear greens grow ten times as tall as the ones here in Wales," she said to me.

"Do they grow more greens?"

"Why, yes! Bushels, and a thousand times more!"

"Do you have places to play?"

"They have the biggest playground near the school, and the ground is the most beautiful *red* earth you ever saw. The streets are laid out in neat rows where many people live. When it rains, the roads are so muddy that you have to wear hip boots."

"Wow! Fun!"

When I was born, my mother had difficulties resulting from a breach delivery. I learned years later that the midwife who helped her during my birth had to force me back in order to make the delivery possible. This brought her to Nome and Kotzebue, so that the damage might be repaired. I don't know the agony felt nor the amount of time spent in readying for the trip and making applications for a Bureau of Indian Affairs travel voucher to enter the government-run Public Health Service hospital, 175 miles northeast of Wales at Kotzebue. This is the only health agency available to Wales people. My brother was taken along, to facilitate the child travel rules, so that he could get his tonsils removed. I was left behind with a neighbor mother who happened to be nursing her new daughter. In later years I was never allowed to forget the time I suckled beside her daughter.

"No wonder you are growing so fast, you enjoyed my milk along with Emily when you were just a baBEEE!"

Thus, my mother and brother Skip were the first in our family to see Nome and Kotzebue. Skip remembers little of the trip, since he was only a boy of two. But my mother brought back photographs of friends, and her memories of the people were probably decisive in my father's final decision to move. As the wife of a man who did not admire gossip, she seldom overplayed the sights she must have seen in Nome. In fact, the good words about Nome came mainly from those who had travelled beyond Nome to places like Fairbanks, Anchorage, and the Lower-Forty-Eight. "There," they would report, "you see and experience fun, excitement, games, women . . ."

Certainly I didn't realize that the "fun" they were talking about was usually some run-down bar, and that their fun almost always ended in the old, old story of the morning after. The big difference between Nome and the outlying villages, is that the villages still continue to some extent the old customs. The villages, with their small populations, do not have many young people, so that the marriageable male has limited choices. In turn, the girls must vie for the few boys. So the adolescent plays the game of disinterest in the girls . . . or boys, while all the time an uneasy courtship goes on.

Eskimo culture of pre-missionary days had a more comfortable method. Agreements were made by the parents so that their offspring would grow up knowing who their future life partners would be, and still be able to partake in the growing-up games all children play, without a word said about grown-up matters. This went on until the time came for marriage, whereupon the customary rules would apply for the brief courtship and the final marriage. Oddly enough, one cannot say that the Eskimo courtship of former days was all that short, even if scholars claim that courtship and marriage involved nothing more than intent and qualifications. For the marriageable young, certain stages were involved in the many learnings preparatory for adult life. This went on through helping the family units daily, through actual work, and even through games. There was no great separation between the young and the old in the old life.

Quite a difference from the situation today. The churches wrestled mightily to liquidate these native practices. Now they place the question of a life philosophy in such a way that it becomes a question of "churches vs. bars and liquor stores." Nome has both in abundance, and the young Eskimo is expected to spend his money by putting some in the offertory plate, and some in the hands of the bartender. Through drunken brawls, he competes with the military personnel, the Nome business men, the prospector, and the construction workers, for the prize of the few girls of the night.

My father had other things to consider: He knew about the dangers in Nome. He was dead set against drinking. There was danger in the possible bad influences upon his children. And there was the other part of Nome life — the unemployment, inhuman poverty, drop-out rates from school, the unspoken but distinct racism which alienates the Nome non-alcoholic. There is also the Nome average middle-class worker, and the overt religious bias against the ignorant but not unhappy Eskimo who is soon identified as unreliable, unimaginative, unproductive, spending his welfare checks on booze, starving his children, and just plain "being an Eskimo."

So Willie Senungetuk weighed the benefits of keeping his younger children near home while they continued their education, against the dangers of such a cataclysmic change as that involved in a move to Nome. If he chose to stay in Wales to continue hunting and fishing, he would also have to be satisfied with village conditions, which even in his time are rapidly being transformed by western technology, not to the benefit of the natives.

Willie Senungetuk and his family prepared to move to Nome.

12

Departure by Bush Plane

The following September, 1951, the Senungetuk family is in the last stages of preparations for the move to Nome. The three older children have recently said goodbye to attend the BIA school in Mt. Edgecumbe. The father has talked with the village schoolteacher, expressing his desire to have the bush pilot, Bill Munz, radioed so that he can pick up the remaining members of the family during the month's end. He knows that communication between Wales and Nome is erratic at best, and wants to be certain.

The amount of money circulating in Wales is so minuscule that the only buyer for the house turns out to be a young man from Little Diomede Island. It is sold for $200, a lot of money exchanged in a village where a child thinks a penny is a great deal, and the village store's costliest item is a hundred dollar rifle which can be "charged" and paid for in a year or two. It is a place where talented carvers of ivory may have to make five cribbage boards to be able to afford the rifle. They don't know that the usual mark-up price would buy the rifle for only one cribbage board in the final consumer's market.

Altogether, Willie's material belongings bring him a little more than five hundred dollars. When he has paid for the bush plane fare, he has a total of one thousand dollars with which to start a completely new life for himself, his wife, and his children.

There are no Great Expectations on the part of the two children, Joe and Cora, about the coming trip. They are vaguely aware of the decision made by the parents, even if indeed they were the main considerations for the move. Since they did not have many toys or clothing for packing, they were not asked to do anything, except to keep out of the way whenever a chance sale of household goods was made. A man might enter the house and ask questions about the family move, and also to see if there was anything he might be able to buy or receive as a gift. He might ask for one good dog, and a price was then quickly agreed upon, somewhere in the area of five or six dollars. Since most of the hunters at Wales already own the necessary number of dogs, they are simply trying to be helpful, since they have always worked things out collectively in other matters. Does this mean the village was a completely serene environment, with no quarrels, no feuding? Hardly; there were times when Wales became virtually a North-South divided community. If the village was a little deeper East-West, there might have been factions accordingly. Wherever there are people, there will be differences. But because Wales is such a small community, feuding parties don't hold their grudges very long. In earlier days, when feuding was not tempered by the intervention of a mixed ideology, it was very honest and direct. In extreme cases, the village ousted unwanted or undesirable persons. Such individuals usually moved to another village. Or if the group as a whole was involved, they made new settlements elsewhere. This may be the reason why the Northwest Alaskan villages had no known history of joining forces to make united villages. Some of the old stories told by the elders are vague memories of how some of the villages came to be. Sometimes it was a story of dispute or argument; sometimes mass starvation or an epidemic upset the leadership. There is no doubt that some of the immigrants to Nome are also modern outcasts from nearby or far away villages. Outcasts to their villages, because of the general strife that comes with living in a village and believing that they are truly more talented and employable than their status implies, while still feeling tied to an area without jobs. Some learn differently, when they arrive in Nome, and see that many other men had the same thought.

There is now a new generation, some full grown and many others very young and trying out the spaces in schoolrooms, the

Nome-born Eskimos. With most jobs in Nome being seasonal, they grow up without knowing the full value of how to live in harmony with their environment and nature — a knowledge and a value owned by their parents. Many have intermarried with other village families. Still others have found the female population in Nome to be very small, because many young girls marry white men, who usually hold better paying jobs. For this Nome-born generation, it is only the beginning of an age totally different from previous generations, one that will last a long time in its effect on the history of the Northwest Alaska Eskimo.

In view of all this, the two younger children were not informed of these hard facts of life, so they made up their own wishes about the journey. And wishes are quickly forgotten by children. The boy is told that he will *ride* one of the bush planes which come to Wales, for the first time! At first he is a little disquieted since this first experience might be too much of a good thing. He might show signs of fear. A possibility. Intermittently, he vacillates from gladness to be accorded such an honor, to being sad that he will soon leave all his friends and his expansive playgrounds.

The bush plane finally arrives. It is a single-engine Stinson painted all over a deep red. In size, it is roughly midway between the smaller Piper Cub and the larger full-wing Beaver. The things Willie has decided to take along for the trip are a few bags filled with clothing and blankets, his trusty old 25-35 Winchester, and whatever family records he has kept. He also takes his treasured items, such as his Schaeffer fountain pen, which has a gold plated band around it, his gold pocket watch, the shoe box of yellowed photographs with torn corners, and his Zenith Transoceanic shortwave radio. His wife brings along her skin sewing equipment, and a few furs she plans to sew into slippers for the curio shops of Nome. Willie wears his only manufactured outer garment, the well-worn brown leather jacket, cut near the waist like an Eisenhower jacket, which he has worn in his younger days, when just married. Underneath, he has on a wool shirt and a pair of longjohns. His pants are the same hunting Levis. His wife wears her colorful parka-cover, since she has not yet had the time to make herself a beautiful squirrel-skin coat. But she has taken along the squirrel furs, trapped mainly at Buck Creek, the summer tin mine camp. The kids wear their school clothes, the boy in his longjohns, a pair of overalls, a cotton shirt, and the mukluks, parka and parka cover. The girl is in homemade bloomers, a tee shirt, dress, parka, and colorful parka cover.

During the loading, the pilot supervises as well as he can, since the family, save for the father, do not know much English. He stuffs most of the smaller items in the rear part of the one compartment for loads. It is accessible both through the small outside door, and through the passenger and pilot compartment. As with the visit of any plane to Wales, the crowd of villagers who have run to the smoothest part of the beach area after being summoned by the cries of the young people, "Airplay! Airplay!", are now milling around or standing by to watch the always exciting possibility of receiving a package or a message. There is drama in the air machine itself, which lands and takes off as if defying the laws of the snow and ice-covered land and sea, the often windy skies. There is now a respect for the thin, painted fabric of the plane, which was until recently used to pencil-mark such messages as "Hi, Mary: Wales. How are you? . . . answered with, "I am fine. Bob, Little Diomede." The Bush pilots learn a certain way of communicating with the villagers only after they gruffly say, "Don't do that!" to some act which might harm the operational features of their planes. It is usually ignored, as if it were a cry over nothing, when the pilot makes a fuss. So the pilots of Alaska, during this period, were the objects of much glamorization. Many stories were told of their adventures with the Eskimos when they themselves were more interested in the financial gains to be had, as the only ties between towns and villages. Even with this monetary aim in mind, they soon grew more and more aware of the fact that they were serving very poor people, who accept them at face value only through ignorance. The bush pilots, in fact, are much revered by the young Eskimo boys, who play with bits of thin board nailed together to make toy airplanes.

Now our pilot throws in more blankets filled with clothing and miscellaneous paraphernalia, tied with rope and string like a tramp's kerchief. This causes Willie to apologize for the large amount of baggage . . . "That's alright, Willie," Munz says, "We'll be able to put some of the lighter things beside them."

This is done and he puts Willie in the front seat, with small Joe in his lap. He packs the rest of the smallest and lightest items near their legs. Finally, he expertly checks the various parts of the plane, the skis, elevators, rudder, prop resistance and so on. He hops in and orders his village volunteer prop-swinger to help him start the engine.

The boy Joe is curious about all the gauges and switches in the plane's cockpit, but he is too shy to ask questions, or even to make a move. He watches the pilot re-enact the motions that he and his playmates have played in fun, pretending to be pilots. Bill Munz has on his amber sunglasses. He wears very simple clothing, quite carefree. Nevertheless, he looks very close to a figure of awe to the Wales people. He wears a pair of good shoepacs, a leather jacket which is not spotted with scratches, a pair of green twill knee breeches, and black leather gloves. He cranks the overhead crank, which creates a strange reaction someplace within the flying machine. He flips switches and checks the readings on the gauges and pushes the throttle, and the propeller spins faster. The plane vibrates and rocks back and forth as the noise level increases. For the boy, it is stangely much quieter inside the plane, than watching it from the outside, where the spectators are pelted with a barrage of noise and snow as the Stinson turns around to taxi to the starting point, where it will take off and not be seen again for another week or two.

The taxiing of the plane, the up-down and sideways motion, the noise, the smell of the airplane, are all new to the boy. He didn't realize it would be so very different being inside instead of outside. He wonders why, at the same time, the interior looks so large and also so small. It just does not fit the plane he has seen so many times before. He didn't realize it would be so bumpy to be riding in it. For the first time in his life, everything immediately surrounding his person is really extraordinary. The fact that he is sitting in his father's lap is unusual. He cannot remember doing it before. He wonders if his father's lap will tire before the trip is over with.

At the revving up of the engine, he is almost startled, but tries not to show it. His father feels his body tensing, and he reassures the boy, saying this is the normal procedure for the plane. He has flown in a small plane before, when he worked for a mining camp around the Kobuk River. The takeoff seems to last a long time in the mind of the boy, if not also in the mind of the pilot. But soon they are in the air.

I don't remember much of what we saw as we flew along the coast towards Lost River, across Grantley Harbor near the town of Teller. Then, across the lower land areas beside the Kiglusik Mountains, to the last leg of the descent between the high hills, just northwest of Nome. There was one time when Mr. Munz circled around the side of a hill to show us a mother brown bear and her cub. I tried with all my might to see them, but since my eyesight was even then not too good, I saw only a blur. We landed on a small field used by the bush pilots of Nome at that time, and my first sight of a town larger than Teller was the gigantic hangar on the field. I thought then they were huge. Now I know they are the smallest hangars I've ever seen since that day.

Pilot Munz helped with the unloading of the plane, and he personally took the trouble of getting his Jeep station wagon, driving it up to the load and helping with reloading the baggage into the vehicle. Then he drove the family to my father's brother's home. Nick Ezukemeow is this man's name.

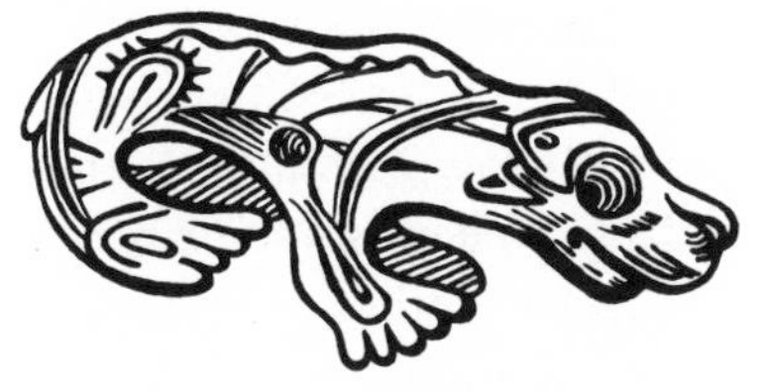

13

"Strange Noises" in Nome

Nick's house is one of those Nome structures built in the late 1930's, after the town's disastrous fire caused the population to build away from the front street business area. In 1951, it appeared to me as a large, not really old house, although the heaving of the permafrost had already buckled the front porch somewhat. Today it looks as if it has given up the strength to keep its right angles, just as the majority of Nome's houses appear. Our first night was a sleepless one for me. Nick's water tank had a pump located in his dining room with an electric motor, which fed an air pressure controlled water pipe system, taking water from a 200-gallon reservoir. This would suddenly turn on and run for about seven minutes every hour or so. It was most unnerving. The other background noises — the hum of the refrigerator, dull roar of the oil stoves, and an occasional passing car, only augmented my wakefulness, even though I knew that the next day would be a good one for sights to see. I didn't mind so much the linoleum floor we were bedded down on, as I did all the strange noises in the dark.

That night was the beginning of events which were to be quite hectic for the next year or so for the family which flew a hundred and fifty miles from one way of life to another, from one culture to another . . . practically from one world to another. Today there are about 2,200 Eskimos in Nome. Omitting the generations born in the town, there must be quite a few who have and still are experiencing similar situations. Of course, all people adapt to strange circumstances every day. Certainly the men and women who moved to Nome from the Lower-Forty-Eight, also had to make some sort of adjustment.

My first experiences with Nome's oddities, according to my ten-year old eyes, were varied and numerous. I noticed that Nome kids were so much more ready to show off toys and abilities than were my former playmates in Wales. I saw that most Nome people walked around heavy-footed and wary of each other or of passers-by. The food was more starchy. There were more eating utensils and the tables were much higher. There were many strange things for a boy of my age, and I found few friends. Our family walked or was driven by Aunt Catherine to friends. Friends they made in Wales, Shishmaref, Teller, Little Diomede Island, King Island and other similar places, through the surface travels of Dad and the men. One of the first families we visited was originally from Teller Mission. This is not really a mission. I suppose it might have been, at one time or another, but I remember it as a desolate area, except for summer camping tents and berries. There was one large building, the estate of a family of millionaires (by Teller Mission standards), also owned by a white man and his half-breed children. They had a large house, a couple of other buildings, probably barns, a speedboat which we campers saw racing to the town side, Teller, across the bay of Port Clarence. I remember the family we visited had a long wooden skiff used for transporting the family to summer camp grounds, and for fishing. The most vivid memory I have of them, are times when they were getting the boat ready to move from their camp to their Teller home. Particularly do I remember the man of the family, when he started up his ancient outboard motor. It was the kind in which you use a forefinger to turn the fly-wheel on top. Once it got going, the racket it made promised more than its performance.

This man has been Dad's good friend all these years. He can't read or write, but he got along by working for the mining company in Nome while it was still operating, and later through help from welfare and by carving ivory, as well as hunting. We first visited his family when he worked for the mining company. His house was then situated between Nome city proper and the East End King Island summer village. It was a small house, even for Nome, and was smaller in total enclosed space than our own modest home in Wales. While the man and woman served tea and crackers, and talked of old times at the summer fishing and berry-picking places near Teller, I made friends with their youngest son, George. He was a couple of years younger than I, and he was eager to talk and to suggest play activities. He showed me his trusty BB rifle and we walked the beach while he gave me a picture of life in Nome. It turned out that he had no playmates in this part of Nome, since he told of having to watch out for those "K.I.s" (King Islanders), whom all Nome school kids looked down on, and who themselves ganged together for protection from other gangs. The other gangs, he said, were: the tough "Jonathan Gang" whose parents came from Shishmaref, the unnamed "Half-Breed" gang of Nome, and other little factions whose origins he did not know. He took great pride in having an older brother to protect him, although he said the best thing to do if confronted by such a gang was to run "like crazy!"

As a ten-year old, I was both heartened and filled with apprehension at his words, as he babbled on of his life in Nome. I was glad there were boys I could play with and listen to, whose families were as "Eskimo" as mine. My misgivings came from the new knowledge of hatred which divided young children into hostile groups. As to George's parents and mine, the things I learned from him were not their concern, since now they were constrained to try and fit into a society which started with employment and survival, in a community that scorned "ignorant Eskimo villagers." As Dad absorbed the minimal knowledge of an illiterate Eskimo from Teller, of the working conditions and opportunities of Nome, I silently absorbed information from this man's son about conditions and opportunities in the school system. For this I gave myself a small promise to try and help these two brothers if they ever needed it, and it was not long before the time came.

It was the beginning of school. The nights were cold and the dirt roads of Nome were frozen solid, with the car tracks becoming ruts of icy mud. The first snows of October were now remaining on the ground instead of melting to form more mud. Soon the snow covered all the ugliness of the dark brown streets, the yellow brown dead grass and the grey board walks. The city D-8 Caterpillar now made its noisy rounds, pushing the white snow into clumps by the sidewalks.

During one recess period at school I stood watching classmates at play on the snow-covered playground. I was not yet accustomed to playing in a restricted area with strange kids. The two brothers were getting ready to return to the classrooms, when I spotted one of them being teased with small clumps of bulldozed snow by a boy from the Kobuk River area. In my awkward English, I told him to stop, and when he asked if it were any of my business, I told him the two brothers were my friends.

"Friends? You don't even deserve friends with your stupid mukluks. You're just a stupid villager!"

I picked up the nearest block of hard snow and threw it at him . . . I hadn't realized I was capable of such angry retaliation. It just brushed his leg. He jumped back, surprised he had moved me to action. The "end of recess" whistle was blown by our teacher and he vowed that he would tell the teacher and the principal of my insolence.

That afternoon, I was asked by the grade school principal to step out of the classroom . . . Once out in the hallway of the reconstructed Army barracks annex to the Nome public school building, he asked me two or three questions starting with "Is it true that . . . " which I answered with a timid monosyllabic "yes" or with a nod of the head. The boy had been true to his word and had told him that I had attacked him with dangerously large snow lumps, for no substantial cause. If he had asked me in Eskimo, I would have at least been able to explain. But, my tongue was tied by his colossal presence in a business suit, his eyebrows twisted in a Super-Principal statement, bearing his monitory yardstick. His final judgment was an order to lean over, which I did not understand at first, since my parents never had sufficient reason to spank me. So he grabbed my neck and shoved it down, at the same time almost breaking the yardstick on my rear with ten loud smacks. He walked off without another word. I stood in that hallway, without knowing what is expected of a punished boy. I opened the classroom door and walked to my desk, sat down bewildered, trying hard to take in what had occurred. My classmates knew I had just been punished. Our teacher had no idea of what had taken place out in the hallway — and there was a quiet which seemed like a roar to me. Finally, I could not restrain my inward pain. I broke out with terribly loud sobs. The teacher asked me to calm down. When I couldn't, she had me stand up in front of her desk to answer questions. Before the entire class, I was subjected to a series of questions, until finally I was allowed to return to my seat.

And so I learned more about the multiplication tables. Listening to a story about "Heidi" without understanding much English, and reading more episodes about Dick, Jane, Sally and Spot and their raincoats, umbrellas, balls, and cement streets, was the extent of knowledge acquired in that classroom.

My father was going through readjustments too. A few lucky incidents led him to an encounter with people whom Uncle Nick knew.

We were bedded down on the dining room floor for the third day. Then, Nick's friend came to visit him. This white man, who had made Nome his place to settle in after coming to Alaska with a military construction crew, owned one of the two "Sanitary Services" of Nome. A good number of Nome businessmen made this civilian-military job a sort of starting point. The U.S. Army did more than establish a military camp in Alaska during the '40's. It left a residue still evident, in the form of people like the man who visited Uncle Nick that night. This man's business enterprises enabled him to buy old houses, to rent to people who do not mind appearances and can pay monthly rents of $30 to $80. While mulling over a game of cards, my Uncle Nick casually asked him if he had a spare house which his brother could buy. Yes, the man had a house he had just acquired; it needed repairing. The price was tentatively set at $1,500 and it was agreed that two payments would buy the house.

We went to see the house the very next day. It had a rear room beside the kitchen, about eight by twelve feet. The kitchen-dining room was about twelve by twelve with a small window facing east. There was an old oil stove between the two doorways to the north rear room. The front room was about twelve by fourteen with a corner divided up for a toilet enclosure, a small clothes closet, and a storm shed. There was a rickety double bed in the front room, a chest of drawers, and a bureau with a mirror. The rear room barely held two Army cots. The kitchen had a cheap table and wooden cabinets. We were enthralled at all the living space. For Dad, it was the best he could afford. We took our belongings, and moved in. We had so few possessions that the house still looked big to us. A sheet of plywood was placed between the two cots in the rear room to make two rooms for Cora and me.

We were there for about four days, when the neighbors introduced themselves by sending their daughter over with a used coffee pot and pan. They were from Kotzebue. The little girl was about my age and she was the first girl I ever saw who had her hair curled. It actually made me stare in wonder. She said, somewhat timidly, but with a voice that I thought was so much more articulate and direct than my friends at Wales, that her parents thought we might need the pots and they would like to meet us soon. So it was my first experience and my first reaction to modern artificial treatment of hair, and fluent English, especially from such a young girl. To my parents it was an act of kindness which they much needed as they strove to fit in to the new social order.

We found that her father worked for the Civil Aeronautics Agency as a local agency carpenter. He spoke Eskimo with the Kobuk area dialect, altogether a new and different one to me, though we could understand almost all of it. It was spoken very rapidly, the sentences ending with a quick upswinging lilt. My father reminisced with him of the Kobuk River land, the hunting and fishing differences and similarities, and laughed over the stories concerning them. Mr. Green (his Eskimo name was Ingnik but he had taken an English surname, as do many Eskimos from the Kotzebue area), was tall and beefy. He had a large family. He must have had some degree of Caucasian blood because his wife was full blood Eskimo and her oldest children by a previous marriage appeared full Eskimo, while their other six children had Caucasian features with brown skins. The youngest two boys were adopted from unmarried daughters and relatives.

My father worked for the mining company soon after we moved to the new house, but since he was an unskilled laborer, was laid off after the dredges were closed down for the winter, with only skeleton crews to keep them running for the following season. He must have really worried about the next job, but he did not show it. He abhorred having to go on welfare of any sort. Yet the winter time in Nome was when the local newspaper's unemployment rate listings began hitting highs of 60-70 percent, along with the growing lists of drunks who had various fines and incarcerations stated beside their names.

We visited families from other villages whenever the house, which was not as large as we thought at first, became a tiresome place. The movie house was practically the only recreational place in Nome at that time, and we hadn't the money to go there. It was during a visit to a family from Little Diomede that Dad learned of a janitorial job open at the school. How to apply? Well, someone could pick Dad up before going to work, and introduce him to the superintendent. There were many applicants, but also many worked for only a week before succumbing to the temptations of the front street bars. What followed such forays was a place in the Nome newspaper drunk list. Most Eskimo men who did not drink had better paying jobs elsewhere, like Mr. Green, our neighbor. Also, the starting pay for a new janitor was about $350 per month, no competition for those who had learned to accept welfare, first as a supplementary income during lean winter months, and then as an easy way out.

So Dad started working, with no references except that from the relative of his Little Diomede friend, and no janitorial experience except for knowing how to follow instructions. He started on the afternoon shift, which ended late at night, and he would come home for a very late supper, tired but glad that he had a job. He would tell about what he had learned so far about his new job — how each man was given sections of the rooms by the chief maintenance man; how much he was learning about the heating and lighting system. And how sloppy the other men were about cleaning the rooms; how some were fired and new men were coming in.

He worked for about four months before it was noticed that he was a diligent worker with a good record of being prompt. They must have learned he had a family he was trying to take care of on the $350.00 monthly pay, in a town where $70-$80 went for oil bills, $10 for electricity, $8 for the sanitary service, $15 for water, and the rest for food and clothing. He was then put on the permanent crew with a $25 raise, and Mom was offered a job as cleaning woman at the superintendent's home. She was quite apprehensive at first since she did not know as much English as Dad, and she was not familiar with the rich trappings of the white family. Anyhow, she was willing to try and augment her sales of fur slippers and mukluks with the extra $40 per month. She always spoke to us, the children, in Eskimo. For the first year in Nome I spoke in Eskimo with her. With all good intentions, she ruined the superintendent's electric coffee maker while trying to wash it clean with the rest of the dishes and it took her a while to find out just exactly what she had done wrong. She mentioned this to her friends who visited us, with a bit of self-criticism, "azukeak!" (how very bad), but always said that she was learning how to do her work efficiently. She would describe to her family the modern housewares she had the pleasure of using. The vacuum cleaner for the rugs. The faucets with hot and cold running water. The matching set of silverware. There were other things she could only admire as she cleaned them. The sofas, fireplace, nicely finished furniture, refrigerator, floor lamps, but I never heard her say that she wished to own such things. Besides the cleaning work, she continued with her sewing of skins and furs, not for the family so much, as for the tourist trade.

From the money she made at the cleaning job, Mom bought raw materials for her sewing. From the little extra she made at sewing, she would treat me to an occasional movie, or give us a little spending money. Or, she would go down town to the few stores to buy something she thought would help us fit more easily into the Nome schools. A new pair of shoes, a scarf for Cora, or maybe a pair of gloves or mittens. She knew that small children dressed in Eskimo clothing were ostracized by others at school. How ironic it was then to be cleaning up a white man's house in order to afford skins and hides to make Eskimo-looking footwear so that she could buy white footwear for her children! And the white footwear, even if fleece lined, felt soled, or whatever was done to make them warmer, were never warmer than the mukluks. I don't recall asking her to buy these things, but I would be very glad when she did. It meant less harassment from the gangs and fewer times that I would go home straight from school, having no desire to play. Sometimes I came home from the playground with bloodied nose or a cut lip, the gift of a couple of boys who made the playground their hunting area for stray village boys smaller than they.

As we settled more and more into the ways of Nome life, our adjustment to it became more and more routine. Before I went all the way through the fourth grade, I qualified for the fifth grade. My sister Cora had just entered the first grade.

Living quarters in the new house at Nome soon became just as cramped as those we had in Wales. I slept in the attic, which was about ten by twelve feet. Maximum head space in the center was about five feet between rooftop and floor. My bed was fitted into the side, where the inside of the roof loomed right above my face when in bed. Next to me was the ladder well, going down into the mini-pantry, a space of about five by five. Also, the oil stove "safety" and stove pipe, the cylindrical water tank and odds and ends of all sorts, vied for space. An adjoining room had a little more head space, due to the truncated crossing of the two roof lines at the front of the house. But there were also more boxes, and a stovepipe, so that the mattress just fit between these.

Soon Dad started the second half of his payments for the house. There was a simple oral agreement between the owner and himself. Usually this was the case in any transaction between a real estate owner and an Eskimo buyer, since there were no accountants or lawyers in Nome. A couple of business secretaries signed documents as Notary Public. A few housewives did the paper work for their husbands. With no business schools for hundreds of miles, this created a sort of monopoly for those who had some idea of how to keep records.

And so events crowded in upon us, and suddenly we found ourselves an Eskimo part of Nome life. I even became accustomed to the "strange noises" of Nome, both physical and ideological.

This was the beginning of the trauma experienced by a Native family as we traveled from our ancient and satisfying life to the strange, unfriendly ways of another world. So completely different was this new world that each day became a completely new experience for all of us.

She learned a little about how profits are made through time saving devices such as the use of different materials for linings.

She also learned how to use a skin sewing machine. Her immediate supervisor was not Mr. Polet, but a part-native who acted as a buffer between himself and the workers. After his death, the shop was sold to a couple from Washington State, and the workers were thinned down to just a couple of sewers. The town newspaper did a great job of welcoming the newcomers as virtual saviors of a nearly traditional Nome establishment. There is no skin sewers' union, and no school for skin sewing in Nome. As young as I was then, I was conscious of the sad fact that each year the quality of Eskimo crafts fell lower and lower. Mr. Polet employed Eskimo women at very low pay. His grandsons were able to attend the University of Alaska, and his family lived very comfortably in one of Nome's few two-story houses. Today the Eskimo craftsmen peddle their wares at the nondescript markets. Mom has the reputation of being a very good sewer, and she keeps busy at her own work.

Besides Nome, Kotzebue is a budding Eskimo town today with an increasing tourist trade, where outsiders come in droves during the summers. I have often wondered where Kotzebue got its name. Now it seems that Kotzebue was an early explorer who must have held his nose while going through Alaska. In Kotzebue, the middle-aged and older folks don their "fancy parkas" and pose for the camera buffs. Out around the countryside those who are less attracted to the tourist dollar wear simple parka covers while fishing or gathering berries. I suppose tourism helps keep the Eskimo traditions alive in an era of technological invasion, by urging the natives to superficial dress and dance. But still I cannot help feeling distressed to know there are some fellow Eskimos who are being exploited because of their innocence in business matters.

As I entered the sixth grade, my brother Skip came home from Mt. Edgecumbe at Sitka, and entered the eighth grade at Nome. Skip came home as a bright young boy, proud of his experience in another world. He was more capable than I was in making new friends, because he had learned through necessity rather than from desire, how to act among strangers. He had many stories to tell of his two years at the Bureau of Indian Affairs regional school.

He talked about the school's dormitory way of life, about his chores such as cleaning hallways and working in the laundry. He was chosen to be a member of the color guard in a school pageant. Indeed he could make friends with grownups as well, and was a favorite of his new Nome teacher, one of only two Negroes in Nome at that time. He and I were about the same height and build by this time, and people would often mistake us for twins. Nevertheless, if we visited his friends' homes, they would know which was which, by his bubbling spirits and my shyness. We were also at an age when we were interested in earning money for ourselves.

Our father was taking on more responsibilities in his work now, to qualify for additional pay. So after school, Skip and I worked and cleaned up a few rooms for him. He paid us five dollars a month. To me, this was much more profitable than a recent try at selling newspapers on the streets. I was so timid that I would sell only about three or four newspapers, with corresponding earnings of fifteen cents or so for an evening's work. I would have to return the unsold newspapers, while other boys were selling their quotas and coming back for more. With the cleaning job for Dad, I was at first so intent at really *cleaning* them, that Skip would complain I was taking so long that it caused us to lose time for other tasks. He figured out a system in which we both had equal work loads and he insisted that I finish on time. Then we would go our ways to spend time with friends, before returning home to do our schoolwork.

During the summers, Skip started working with the local plumber. He would saunter around in his dirty overalls, sometimes so sooty that it would take a lot of precious water to clean up. At home, we also had the task of washing dishes and keeping up our sleeping quarters. We ironed our own clothes if we wanted them pressed, and we had now grown to like a neat appearance for school, in the whiteman's way. We ordered clothes from Sears with the money we earned. Our father had grown acquainted with the ways of the Eskimo in Nome, and he began to do some hunting and fishing in his spare time. So we had Eskimo-type food, which we ate at the family table to augment the starchy foods bought from the local stores.

One incident which is evidence of our eating habits occurred when I was still in the sixth grade. Sometimes we had dried fish and seal oil for a hurried lunch, and this we did one Friday. In the afternoon, I went back to school and found that I had not washed my hands and lips well enough to remove the fish and seal oil smell. The class was scheduled to go through a new course in dancing, and we were herded to the gymnasium to try the foxtrot and other social wonders. When the instructor found that the boys were too shy to ask the girls, she had the *girls* choose the partners. Some of the girls whom I had only looked at in admiration before, were now showing eagerness in teaching me the intricacies of the dance. All through that blasted hour, I was more than just shy — I was dreading the consequences, if they completely swore off contact with an Eskimo boy who only wanted to fit into their non-Eskimo world, and who *smelled.* If there were Eskimo girls alone in my class, I would not have had to worry. But my class consisted of a majority of Eskimo boys, and a small number of mostly white girls.

Most of Nome's vehicles are pickups. There are a few station wagons, Jeeps, Scouts, and other smaller cars. The school superintendent had a Plymouth sedan which he used to go out to the country to hunt ptarmigan. Sometimes he asked Dad to come along with him, and they usually came back with their limit in a morning's hunting. At this time Dad began to think about owning a vehicle. Like many Eskimo men who come to Nome and have a steady job, he saw the advantage of owning some means of transportation, even though the dirt roads did not go very far in the early 1950's. In fact, the roads ended at Council, a dead mining village, some 65 miles east of Nome. But the fishing and hunting camps were anywhere from four to forty miles out of town. Each year the closer camps yielded less and less game, due to more and more Eskimos acquiring cars to set up fishing camps. When we first came to Nome, I can remember there were a lot of ptarmigans, squirrels, owls, field mice, and rabbits around. At this time the fish and game laws were concerned with the big State income producers, such as the salmon runs on the Southeastern part of Alaska, the big game animals such as the moose, bear, sheep, goat, and the migratory ducks and birds. In the late '50's there was a cry of "Unfair!" from the Eskimos of the Kotzebue and Pt. Barrow areas, when an Eskimo hunter was charged with shooting ducks out of season. They felt that the fish and game laws catered to the Lower-Forty-Eight duck hunting seasons, without realizing that the same migratory birds did not arrive at their northernmost nesting grounds until the duck hunting season in the southern states was well over with. A small protest occurred when some hunters shot a duck out of season each, and turned themselves in to the local game warden, who had charged the first man with "out of season hunting."

When Dad wanted to keep up his tradition of hunting and fishing, he knew he had to have a car. So after we had been in Nome for three years, he negotiated for the sale of a Dodge ¾-ton pickup, 1947 model. He bought it with $500 cash. Once the truck was delivered to our non-yard (a bit of mud, gravel, tundra grass, beside the dirt road), he was at a loss as to how to learn to drive it.

He was told by a neighbor how to operate the shift stick and the clutch, and so he began to drive without further instruction. He would take us to Uncle Nick's camp site, going the full speed of 19 miles an hour. Young men whose families had already learned through a generation of car-driving would pass by, yelling insults. Within a few months, he was able to drive at the allowable speed limits. He still drives with the first-learned two hands tightly gripped on the steering wheel. I was always intrigued by his fast movements while executing tight turns. He didn't allow his hands to cross on the wheel even then.

He also paid $400 for a summer cabin on skids, which was then situated on a more exclusive camp site about seven miles northwest, called Dexter. This area was used by white campers who liked rod fishing. There the cabins were often much better equipped than many of the Eskimo homes in Nome. A couple of cabins even had electric plants, fireplaces, and garages. The one Dad bought was owned for a short while by an elderly lady who ran a community center. But like many social organizations in poor areas, her teen-age club, girls' sewing clubs, and rummage sales, only provided a drop in the bucket for the community center, while she lived comfortably without criticism from anyone. Since she had sacrificed her summer cabin to Dad, she felt she was entitled to have him do jobs such as hauling sand for her cat. Dad would ask me to help him take the truck and drive out a couple of miles to the beach with a couple of shovels. Generally, her request came just as the fall freeze began, and it was a bitch to find the loose dry sand. So we filled up the giant cardboard box with sand and lugged it up in smaller boxes to her apartment above the community center.

The cabin was not doing Dad any good at Dexter, so he paid the local trucking company to drag it down with a tractor to its present site at Fort Davis, for about $150.

Unlike the Dexter camping site, Fort Davis is a camp which cries out its lack of material affluence, even in its overall appearance. Most of it is comprised of tent frames, such as the ones we used in Buck Creek at the tin mining camp. Usually a ten by twelve heavy duck canvas tent is used for the wooden platform for the floor and base of the permanent frame. Then there are the five or six wooden and sheet metal cabins, not much larger than the tents. Each camp is equipped with the merest necessities. The wood stove for the cabins suffices, and usually a half oil drum fitted with stove pipes, is used for the tents. To keep the tent from the hot stove pipe, a wire is bent into a "safety," shaped like a daisy, and sewn to the tent cloth. The ubiquitous Standard Oil kerosene container box is used for camp furniture, makeshift cupboards, grub boxes, and work tables.

For all the impoverishment that shows through the people and the buildings of the city of Nome, the poverty as it appears in a fish camp cannot readily be dismissed as a final determination of the state of the Eskimo in Nome. A family that can afford the tent, the fishing seine, the boat, and the camping gear, is in fact a happy family that can make use of the native instincts of living off the land. And so the months of June, July, August, and September are celebrated by men such as Dad, as a time when they can still feel a part of the ages-old traditions from which they came. To catch a sufficient supply of fish at the camps near Nome, is hard work. First of all, one spends a lot of menial labor through low-paying unskilled work, to save enough for the material used. The cheapest seine net runs to about fifty dollars without floats and weights, rope and repair materials. The rowboat amounts to another hundred dollars. Accessories for the boat: oarlocks, oars, motor, gas tanks, costs another two hundred dollars. Hip boots, clothing, and transportation to the camp site are also costly. Once these items are acquired, there is the matter of their upkeep. Indeed, it often becomes questionable as to whether "subsistence fishing" is practical. Usually, those who spend week-ends and summer vacations at Ft. Davis are the older Eskimos and their infant grandchildren who need to be looked after. The young people are in Nome, not really learning anything, except the futility of labor in a ghost town.

In this manner, the typical Nome Eskimo family today is split, not only into a generation gap, but into widely separated age groups. The infant grandchildren, a good number of them illegitimate, are raised from toddlers to school age by their grandparents, in the most Eskimo way possible. Then comes the inevitable tragedy — the schooling which excludes their grandparents' life style, the classmates who are quick to make stabbing judgments, and the general apathy of the whole community. All these factors hit the youngster a blow upon his most sensitive spot, his pride and the good memories of the quiet days at the fish camps. Good days, with fresh, clean air, outdoor games, kindness in relationships, and some degree of security. Thus the youngster is almost doomed to relive the same breaking-away point that his young parents have experienced some fifteen years earlier. There is no explosion of tempers, no irate parents who write to editors or try to let congressmen know of the problem. No newspapers dwell upon the problems of the Eskimo youth. There is only the silent antagonism shown by the campers, who feel that they are themselves doomed to extinction as a hunter-fishing people.

In truth, the Eskimo youth wants the best of both cultures: his ancestral culture, and that of the Western society. On one hand, he feels cheated because both cultures are tearing at him and he has no standards on the basis of which he can make good choices. And on the other hand, he sees mainly the negative side of the Eskimo culture, and cannot fail to see the negative side of the European-based culture. His best instincts tell him that it must be possible to blend the two. Young, impatient, lacking in education and opportunities, who can blame him if he finds himself in a corner and cannot choose wisely!

15

Struggle for Survival

Survival is a major problem for the Eskimo family in Nome. In the course of the past 17 years, my father has indeed managed to survive. He is certainly not a man of means with prospects of ease and comfort in his later years. Still, he has been able to accumulate all that he feels is good for the "complete hunter-fisherman." Two camps, a skinboat, a gill net, a shotgun, three rifles, a new pickup truck, accessories and tools required for upkeep. These are the worldly goods of a man who has spent half a century in sheer struggle for existence. For a Nome Eskimo, however, this is the inventory of a successful man, one who has been able to hold both sides of his culture. As to Dad's camps, the amount of time spent is so short, it would seem that all that effort was at least partially wasted, since the equipment sits through November, until the spring months of April and May.

Willie uses his equipment not only for himself, but for the other people who come to him for help. Some have spent their last dollar for a bottle of cheap rot-gut. Some are not complete families, those in which the widows and divorcees often cannot make ends meet with the welfare checks. Others have not understood the usefulness of encouraging their children to further education. He sees them all as people who need help, and when they receive help from him, he cannot expect to be repaid except in friendship. He has also recently learned that it is questionable as to whether he has legal ownership of his campsites. The Bureau of Land Management gives permission only to remain on the site temporarily, to hunt and fish in those areas which are not used for commercial purposes and not claimed by whites. This means he can be kicked out if anyone bothers to look under his camp sites, finds minerals, and decides to develop the site for commercial purposes.

With so much of Alaska now viewed as a haven of natural resources, this is not impossible. It would be the ultimate in the process of breaking down men like Dad, who have managed to stay within the orbit of merely satisfactory conditions. To me, it would look much like the genocide that describes America's historic treatment of natives, since my father would probably just succumb to the law, because of his age and lack of opportunity to go on to other things.

I look back at my experiences at the Fort Davis camp with a sense of both sadness and fulfillment, as part of a time when I also had to fill in application blanks for college and federal employment. (What is your hobby (ies)? — "hunting and fishing.") I have mused that this would have been a loaded question for Willie to answer, since his main occupation was in fact, "hunting and fishing," which he had to relinquish for the opportunity to push the broom so that he could hunt and fish "in spare time." The sadness, if not the complete despair of the situation rests with his inability to look at hunting and fishing as a sport, knowing that his people are tied to it like a mistreated dog on a leash. On the other hand, affluence and vacation spots flourish in other areas of the United States, including Alaska. People can *buy* fresh air and relaxation by the day, week, or month.

Many of the hunting and fishing implements used by the Northwest Alaskan Eskimos for winter, early spring and late fall are not much changed. Since there are not many salmon runs beyond Nome, the seine net is not an old fishing device. Neither are the rowboats and related equipment. The gill net is neither old nor new, since the trading of twine allowed its introduction to villages above Nome at an earlier date than that of the seine. Uncle Nick already had his camp when we moved to Nome, and his wife was the one who taught Mom and Dad the fine art of seine fishing. Uncle Nick is a teetotaler while Aunt Catherine likes to enjoy a senseless binge every once in awhile. However, when the fish start their run in the summer, she is certainly a match for any fisherman in Fort Davis. Catherine is very much admired for her fishing skills, when she is not "uptowk"-ing, as my parents say, or "uptowning." She and Uncle Nick had an old panel truck which she learned to drive after tearing up its transmission by suddenly shifting it in reverse, a fatal mistake for the fourth gear position. She would pile her children on the panel truck and drive down to Fort Davis, sometimes to handle the heavy seine and flatbottom all by herself while Nick was working.

He was a carpenter for the mining company. When it closed down, he did odd jobs for awhile before becoming a truck driver for the local water delivery companies. There are usually two or three such companies offering work during the winter, when the summer water pipes for the city are drained. He has probably worked for all of them, since they change hands frequently when the owners decide to sell out and move to warmer climates, or expand to more profitable business ventures. I don't know how much younger Nick is than Willie, but he looks older, with his short-cropped pepper and salt hair, his usually toothless mouth, and his wrinkled face. He hates to wear his dentures because "they are more trouble than their worth."

I spent many afternoons, many week-ends at Fort Davis, time spent away from the usual pursuits of a young man in the city. I really did not fit into either scene, anyhow. But while I was at Fort Davis, and later at the next camp that Dad built further down the coast, I always looked forward to being with Nick. Whenever I arrived, my uncle would look up from what he was doing — playing solitaire, readying for a rowboat ride up the river, filling up a fuel tank, working on a motor, or some such task — and give me that greeting which no one can ever do better to make me feel so welcome. The most genuine smile even without teeth, without a neat haircut, without neat anything — just a neat smile. "Ohhh, HeLOOO YOOOsef! HOW's the BOY?" Then he would go on, without my asking, to tell me the prospects of the day. "Yesterday, I went up to the third bend and there was a lot of . . . " Or, "fishing is not too hot around here this morning; maybe if I go on up the river, I can find out if they are going up or sticking around further on down . . . " He was always ready to give me pointers as to where the game might be, and when it would be the best time to hunt. He always accompanied Dad on the skinboat hunting trips; at least when he was not working.

There were many times when I went with him to hunt ptarmigan, duck, and seal. Most of these hunts were unfruitful, although they were certainly good lessons for me. At that time, I thought that hunting and fishing involved nothing more than getting up early and being at the right spot at the right time. There was the time when he walked nearly thirty miles in knee deep fresh fallen snow for ptarmigan. He was to show me the places where they usually roosted on low bushes during late fall, but most of the time I was seeing his tracks in front of me and trying to step into them. They were too far apart for my slower snow-walking pace. Going uphill, I found myself wishing he would soon tire and take a rest, but he kept going. Yet, he was the one who would ask me, out on the seal hunts, if I was warm enough, or hungry, or if I wanted a grown man's permission to do the next shooting.

There were a few other boys whose parents camped at Fort Davis, who enjoyed the company, and the freedom from Nome city life. I met them whenever they themselves were not busy helping their parents, and we would talk of the experiences of the previous catch. We were also rod and reel enthusiasts; or more so than our parents. There is always a lot to learn about this type of fishing, in which the fish do not always gather at the same places every year. When I first started to fish with a rod and reel, much of it was just trying to snag the salmon and trout, which had other things in mind than nibbling on a fish egg. This was at a time when the mouth of the Nome River was very deep and narrow, and the fish were easily seen. Since then, the annual change of the river mouth has made it a wider, shallower one, in which more enticing bait is needed. Much of the gravel and sand near the mouth has been steam-shovelled and transported to the expanding roads further and further away from Nome. We would compare rods or reels and then vow that the next money saved through summer or part-time work would go for the better tackle.

Whatever it was that we youngsters did, I think it was done at least in part in order to forget the conditions in Nome, at a place where there were no tourists and no curious whites. No foreigners bothered to come close to the outwardly unkempt camp site. Just the same, there was a sort of order about the camps when one had the chance to visit them often enough. An order more felt than seen. The order of something which may not be felt or seen in the next generation, the order of a way of life which has been pushed out by such places as Nome.

Willie has tried to make his camp sites as comfortable as possible. He is aware of the differences in values of the Nome white and the Nome Eskimo more than most of the natives of Nome. He is in contact with teachers who are responsible for educating the new generation of Eskimos, and he learns what the teachers criticize most. To him, some of these criticisms embody virtual gems of instruction for the dying Eskimo culture. He probably does not realize that these "gems" cover up gross misunderstandings, the result in part of a high teacher turnover situation. The constant changes in the teaching staff guarantees that no far-reaching solutions will be dealt with. The most common complaints have been: the Eskimo school kids are too dirty, too poor, too uninvolved in protection of school property, too unaware of social graces, and too unmindful of the benefits of higher education. Therefore, when Dad started to set up a second camp at Nook, he wanted to make it as "white" as possible. He installed insulation and inside walls. He put in windows on all four sides and covered the exterior with tar paper. He laid a linoleum floor and trucked down the better discards from our Nome house. Uncle Nick helped him with the finer aspects of carpentry needed on the front steps and storage cabinets in the storm shed. It is really a small place. But to Dad it is his pride and joy; his answer to all that he heard in the school about the backward Eskimo, an answer that states there is no such thing as a "backward" Eskimo race.

Willie completed the Nook camp at the age of 61, and his physical condition has slowed down enough to show. Even then, he bought things to make himself self-sufficient in doing the jobs around the two camps. For instance, he used his new geared hoist to haul up his sixteen-foot flat-bottom boat to high ground, from the lagoon beach. He had tied one end to a driftwood post with the nylon rope attached to the hoist, and the other end to the hemp rope of the boat, apparently convinced that the old hemp rope could take the strain of the pull.

It was a nice cool autumn day; everything was still. The dead grass and tundra shrubs seemed to be waiting for the time they would be afforded the protection of the new snows, which was about a month away. Patience is the by-word for everything on the tundra, except for my father, who is laboring away to put things in their places for the winter. He has had a full summer of enjoying the boating and the quiet days, puttering away on the things that have to be done so that another summer will be assured. I was just out of the Army, another chapter in his years during which his children have been away one place or another, away from his life, his world. Anyhow, I was trying to make myself helpful around the camp, but he was too set in his ways, no longer relying on anyone but himself to do the things he felt were necessary.

I had just fetched water for cleaning some fish I caught when I looked over to see what Dad was doing. He was getting the rope tighter and tighter on the homemade winch, and the rope, straight as an arrow, began to pull the heavy boat an inch at a time. Then it happened! WHAPP! Like a .22 pistol shot, the hemp broke and he fell back. In that split second, I saw the rope whipping back directly at him. I ran to him, but he got up by himself and stood erect. That was a moment when I realized how strong a mind and body can be if forced to be pitted against so much. The three-quarter-inch rope had glanced off his cheek and hit full force on his shoulder, but he gave no sign of pain. He just smiled in a sort of embarrassed manner while I helped him drag the boat up in the old way. We put driftwood logs underneath and rocked it up the beach. To me, the quiet air became a few degrees colder as we went about our business and the night grabbed the day as we drove home.

All those years of living with my parents could not make me comprehend more of the fact that it had been a hard life for Dad, than at that moment, when the test of not only the rope, but of the man and his environment was suddenly thrust before me. And yet, there was nothing really resolved from the incident. I could not really help my parents re-do their lives. Not that they would want it re-done, because the years went by without rendering them helpless, and they are happy. Neither was this the first time that a close call happened in our family. Stoicism is not really the special characteristic of an Eskimo family. If Dad is the no-nonsense realist who can treat his children's mistakes with angry scolds, our Mom is the one who can take the delinquent aside and quietly suggest better things to do. She once fainted at the sight of vomitus, when I had my tonsils taken out. For Dad, it probably is a hold-over from the times when he had to vie for a position as sole provider for a family amid no-nonsense fellow hunters. But, that veneer of toughness and stern determination falls apart as readily as it is put on, as can be witnessed in his treatment of his grandchildren. No grandchildren below the age of five or six can escape his doting, almost childlike praises and playing. Also, close friends, white or Eskimo, can always recall his bursts of laughter and joking which can totally erase his moments of seriousness to a point of finding him a truly great friend to know.

But, besides grandchildren and close friends, I think that his sons would have a different definition for what is known as a close filial relationship, than those we read about in the school books, view in movies, or observe in other family situations. We cannot say that he was grouchy or unfair. Neither can we say that he was cruel, for he hardly ever touched us in anger. If there was praise for us, it was usually in the form of "Tdushza, Knunnuk adtah tdaimunna khiziennic inoonadtook." Roughly translated, it means, "Here it is readily comprehensible, because here now this example for its worth is the only one which proves the way to live in the past and future."

Ever since he started to work for the school and began to get free passes to the basketball games, he has become a great fan of Nome's most important school sport. When Skip and I entered high school, I was elected to the team because of my height, and Skip became its manager the first year. Mom and Dad watched every game, and when we came home after the games before going back to the school janitor's room to sleep (Skip and I were also "elected" to sleep near the furnaces to keep watch over them), Dad would give the strangest type of basketball criticism and proposed stratagems any youngster could hope to hear. Half in Eskimo and half in English, he would describe the bad plays, and then proceed to give suggestions on what might be done the next time. One could almost translate these observations from his memories of the times when he was young, and participated in the Eskimo games.

One Eskimo game was a form of kickball, in which a sealskin and reindeer hide ball, filled with reindeer fur, was furiously kicked about on the ice for points, by unlimited teams. He remembers the time when he damned near broke his toes on a hapless opponent's leg. He must have been newly married at the time, because Mom remembers the agony he suffered from this sport. I was never really good at any sort of athletics. The Nome high school team went through four years without making any spectacular record, and my team mates and I went through four years of discouraging attempts at keeping up the once championship material of ten years before. The team had just been entered into the Class B tournament bracket when I started playing. The last year, we were admitted to Class A. Throughout the tourney years, we were first beaten by the City League, whose players were the championship alumni. We had to fly to such cities as Fairbanks, Anchorage, Seward, and Valdez to be beaten some more. We were beaten in more ways than by just playing a game with other high schools. Our first and second string teams were comprised of about half full-Eskimo boys and half mixed Eskimo, and white.

The Eskimo boys, myself included, were not always completely sold on the idea of aggressive offense in the play of basketball. We expended our energies, not because of wanting so much to win the lopsided games, but from wanting to fit into the kinds of activities that the cities had to offer young active boys. I don't know how many eyeglasses I went through while playing basketball. Some of the nights that Skip and I spent at the janitor's room were spent, at least to a small extent, in washing underwear and athletic socks after brotherly quarrels dealing with smelly socks and accusations of laziness. We bought new basketball shoes every year. The rest of the team were not always so fortunate, and we gave our old pairs to some of our team mates whose shoes looked as if cherry bombs had exploded in them.

There were other activities in our high school days besides the annual trauma of Alaska's most popular sport. Skip and I, like our father, didn't miss work except for five or six days due either to illness or excessively stormy weather. We managed to graduate in the top third of our class, even if we didn't try as hard as we could have. However, there were other things we took part in that took time away from our studies. There was the high school band; Skip opted for the trumpet and promptly ordered one from Sears. I was given the instrument that was too heavy for anyone else — the baritone saxophone. It was so old that I was continually ordering parts for it through the school. Once, I even went to the trouble of fixing a needle spring for one of the keys by soldering on one of my mother's skin sewing needles.

Then there was the Teen Club, occupying the old Army barracks, which was fitted with a few chairs and a phonograph. Even as I noticed that a good percentage of the white girls were not allowed to attend these weekly dances, I grew to like mingling with my classmates, and enjoyed the jitter-bugging with no special girls. Although some of the boys were too shy to try out the new dances (Like Skip was, quite unexpectedly), the affairs were always terribly lopsided in the boy-girl proportions, with boys in the majority. This was due mainly to the Eskimo and white families who mistrusted any contact of their daughters with Nome's teenage boys. The reason for this attitude on the part of the Eskimo parents was usually due to the fact that they took literally the teachings of the churches. As to the white parents, there seems to be no identifiable reason except racism and prejudice, of which there was plenty in Nome.

The high school years for Skip and me were most enlightening. We began to understand why Dad wanted us not to relent in our progress towards graduation. We felt how fortunate we were to be working. We were also finding out that the old fundamentalist taboos of no smoking and no drinking that Dad had wrapped around us were not binding forces. One form of release came because of the arrival of Ron and Nancy from Mt. Edgecumbe; I remember how aghast I was to see them sneaking cigarettes and smoking them secretly. At first (at the age of 13), I felt that they were committing the ultimate rebellion. Then I found out that Mom and Dad knew about this. Mom's point of view was that they should not smoke, but if they really wanted to, they should make their argument known to Dad, as to why it was alright to smoke. They kept sneaking cigarettes anyhow, not wanting to gamble on a successful reason why it was "all right" to smoke. I was just starting into my teens when all of the traumatic experiences began to happen between a hard, non-drinking, no nonsense, non-smoking father and his children, who were much like any other young people.

The differences between my parents' ages and that of their growing children, were really differences between opportunities open to each generation. Such differences caused the least friction, however. Mom and Dad never wished to make big issues, and I truly believe they tried hard to understand. But from 1954 on, there were other and more profound issues that shook the foundations of the Senungetuk family. Such issues were brought about because the young people realized that cultural assimilation was de facto taken for granted by the older people of Nome, both white and Eskimo. It was taken for granted that business opportunities existed only for the whites, and that the Eskimos were in their natural place at the bottom of the opportunity ladder. The older white people were of course advocates of the status quo, mainly because no one objected to the system, and those who were the main money exchangers dealt not only with Nome business men, but with outside companies such as those in Seattle. For example, Hunt and Mottet (plumbing and heating equipment) of Seattle, 2,000 miles from Nome, has a virtual monopoly over Nome's pipe supply, tools, and other hardware. They are certainly not the best or most economical merchandisers, but they have long standing as suppliers. The same is true of many other important products such as building materials, motors and parts, tractors, road graders, boats, and automobiles.

Seattle is probably well satisfied with the steady income from Alaska's stand-still economy, knowing that there is no reason for this income to lapse. Indeed some day there may be an increase, from such items as the oil discoveries in Alaska. During the years of working at Nome Plumbing and Heating, Nome Hardware, Nome Public Schools, Federal Aviation Agency, and the Lomen Commercial Company, Skip, Ron and I have been closer to the operations of small community business than, say, our father. So the differences between the attitudes of the older generation and the younger involve much more than the educational status of both. We start to form our own ideas of what a business in Nome is, and we find that these ideas do not conform to Dad's. He maintains that the business district of Nome is the mainstay of Alaskan life, no matter who is running these businesses, or how they are run. Alaskan life to him is still centered around his immediate surroundings, even if he may be vaguely aware of middle-American life elsewhere. We, his sons, are at a point where we see so much being squeezed out of friends, relatives, and other Eskimos . . . and we have to disagree. Vast changes are needed in business, labor, education, management, and as well in the position of our own people in the economy of the state.

We argue about the usefulness of the church, while Dad believes there is nothing bad at all with a Nome church, even if there are some questionable practices by the more fundamentalist ones.

I don't think Dad fully understood what was taking place in the world of his teenage sons, even if he was aware of certain problems. What I felt then as a separation of the former closeness of the family was probably just his desire not to interfere with the teaching of his sons, education and training which he did not have at a similar age. Even his hard line principles of no smoking or drinking, which wore down to subtle lines of example, I sort of missed, because he just did not address himself to us any more than he had to. Sometimes, he would say something to *all* of us, if he found out that *one* of us had done something wrong. Naturally, we felt that this was grossly unfair. But we were still very wary of getting him angry.

Anger, to Dad and other Eskimo elders, is quite a different type of emotion than what is popularly seen in movies, books and other non-Native circles. There is no mistaking his anger for any other emotion. If he has a deep underlying silent rage against the present conditions of his modern day society, he does not show it.

Today, there are younger generations. Their emotions are less contained than those of my father. Willie's children are more than satisfied with his silent courage in dealing with the new world. Perhaps the youth will accept this heritage, adding to it their own eloquent, articulate solutions.

The Eskimo and His Art

In these next few pages, the author presents some of his work as an artist. He is but one of many Eskimo artists whose imagery, closeness to the environment, and love for his land combine with more modern skills and technology to produce and continue to produce the Art of the Eskimo.

No culture survives without its Native arts. Once that is gone, all is gone. Eskimo arts are damaged, sometimes distorted, often vulgarized, but they are alive.

The arts of the Native have suffered immeasurably from foreign intrusion. Part of this deplorable result is due to the impoverished situation of the Eskimo people, so that the manufacture of so-called "crafts" items for the benefit of tourist sales, has taken precedence over the loving care with which the arts were produced in days before white contact.

This writer believes that a great revival of Alaskan Native arts is in the making. However, there must first of all be a revival of learning, an understanding of the culture of the people and of the place of art in their lives. "Alaskan Art" is today understood to be a collection of landscape paintings of snow-covered mountains, posed animals in realistic settings, and portraits of bush pilots. Pure junk, most of it!

This book was designed to present an individual statement on the arts and the life of one part of Alaska, in the hope of bringing about new, fresh approaches to a struggling but not yet dead culture.

WHO LISTENS . . .

When the Native Raises His Arm or His Voice?

(water color)

Shadow of Oil Resource

Few places on earth have the natural resources of Alaska. Minerals, oil, and all of nature's bounty is here. The recent discovery of Alaska's oil potential for profit has brought about the complete debasement of human desires. Greed, jealousies, the pulling and tugging of giant corporations and individuals . . . all these stand in the shadow of this state's enormous oil resources.

The Northwest Alaska Native is uneasy. How should he react? Are there indeed new employment opportunities? Does he have the right to surrender the land of his ancestors, land which belongs to his descendants as well?

The young but able Alaska Federation of Natives has become a strong voice of Native concern. At issue is the whole future of a once quiet, expansive land, rich in many other resources besides oil — including the resource of human beings.

On the facing page, the four-color wood block print illustrates the author's reaction to the question of Alaska's most recent and most lucrative resource discovery. **"Emergence of Resource — the Oil Spill Shadow,"** is meant to express the utter despair, felt by this writer in the mere contemplation of the construction of the Alaskan oil pipeline. It would destroy the land, the people, and the environment.

Shamanism: Historic Eskimo Religion

Throughout the history of Man, the great religions of the world have dealt with everything in society; from the setting up of trade barriers, controlling beliefs, developing prejudices, or encouragement of knowledge and a belief in Man's higher instincts. Shamanism among the Eskimos was a religion. It was one form of religion, to be sure, but it was effective for our way of life. When Christian religions arrived, the Eskimo religion was rejected and fought, as a "savage" phenomenon.

As soon as the Eskimo accepted Christianity, certain fanciful, inaccurate, and strictly imagined properties were assigned to Shamanism. Such as the Ahnagotkok passing through a crack in the wall, being swallowed up by the earth, or summoning up the deceased.

More accurately, Shamanism encompassed the belief that spirits inhabited animals and inanimate objects; that a chief deity was an Old Woman who lived in the seas; and that two spirits resided in a man's body — one that is transferred to a new-born child after the man's death (whereupon the child was given his name), and the other spirit being destined for the Land of the Souls. The poetry and music, the story telling and legendry of Shamanism are not recognized. The Eskimo religion was part of the life of the people, part of the arts, medical practice, a system of psycho-therapy which is only now being "discovered" by modern science.

On the facing page: "The Shaman's Visions," three-color wood block print.

Lost Tales of Eskimo Symbolism

The title of the three-color wood block print on the facing page is:

Ting-Myak-Puk: The Large Bird.

As the artist worked to bring this print to life, he visualized a great bird, and a human being in the foreground. The bird, and the environmental emanations seem to tell the man: "This is your land. Do not go beyond it. This is where your life is. This is where you belong."

Only felt by the artist, are the many ancient stories of warnings not to go beyond the Tree Line . . . stories of legendry and religion embraced as one. And, although some have violated the warnings of the Ancient Ones, and have indeed ventured beyond "the Tree Line," sooner or later they return to their land and their homes.

In the Twentieth Century,
Where Goes the Spirit of the Shaman?
(Lithograph and Colored Ink)

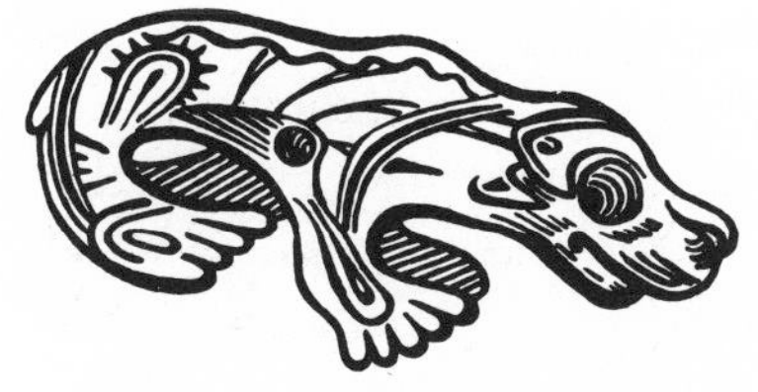

16

Civilization and its Problems

One of the first violations of Dad's wishes by Skip and me occurred while we were attending a basketball tournament at Fairbanks. It involved what was to be our first taste of booze. A rather funny incident then, but the first bad taste of beer had already happened by way of our team mates, who sneaked in a case of beer through a window. In the next few years we completely familiarized ourselves with the Alaska Eskimo-Booze experience. It was no longer a strange potion sold to many a neighbor and drunk by many a classmate. Skip had drunk about three-quarters of a can of beer and I had only a sip when he convinced me to take it, so that I could not tell on him. He became a little talkative, and I went to sleep that night thinking "maybe I did feel it a little," with that one awful-tasting sip.

Besides the first beer-tasting, there was the first smoke with the resulting first coughs; and then the half-pint vodka bottles which friends hid beneath their jackets or under their belts, and sneaky little nips taken here and there, ("mickeys" the nips were called). In Nome, there is nothing — but absolutely nothing except one movie house, a small six-lane bowling alley which had to be subsidized by the city to keep it from going bankrupt, the bars, the churches, and the winter basketball games. But we could take carefree rides into the country and fish, or hunt ptarmigan.

In winter, we could go cross-country skiing, ice fishing, bowling (if we could afford it), and attend many events which became childish after awhile, such as the Civil Air Patrol, the Boy

Scouts, and parties. A young person is expected to grow up very rapidly in Nome, and when he gets to be a certain age, he is dropped from one age group to the next, not because of pressure from members of the group, but due to his own capabilities. The few social organizations of high school age groups are very cruel to those who may feel they are too old for activities such as school dances and popcorn concessions at the school games. This is the critical period for the young people of Nome, as it is in other places. The high school drop-out finds himself with exactly nothing to look forward to, except the dregs of jobs, always waiting to be filled by workers who won't cry because of the low wages. He may become a sweeper for the local movie house whose owners feel they must divide the work to employ as many poor Eskimo boys as possible, besides saving on permanent pay for a maintenance crew; or as a dishwasher for the few restaurants; or be a delivery truck driver; a stock boy for the bars; a hospital janitor or dishwasher; or an airport receiving and shipping clerk.

All these jobs at Nome are either minimum wage scale, or even less. There is no labor union protection in such jobs, and there is no hope to work oneself up in the "ranks," because each higher ranking job is already filled by someone who has learned to do his utmost to keep the job. Mere subsistence is what such a job offers, moreover. A man is usually a jack-of-all-trades, a full-time helper, who will do everything the movie owners ask — whether it be delivering film cases from the airport, groceries from the docks to the apartment of the owner, or acting as "strawboss" for the kids who sweep the place and shovel snow from the front door. The restaurant cooks and waitresses are usually full-time employees; they are imported. The store managers are also imported from places like Seattle, Anchorage, or Fairbanks. When they get tired of Nome or their daughters are old enough to be looked at, they are shipped out and again another family is imported.

Bartenders are usually permanently employed people who find it almost impossible to keep order in a place where people rarely go to have just one drink. They are probably the best paid workers in Nome, besides the few permanent jobs in the other service-related jobs.

The airport and hospital may get all sorts of underlings to work full-time or part-time, but they also have their permanent staff of maintenance men. Aircraft mechanics are much in demand in Northwest Alaska. Again, there is no school nearby for the indigent native to learn the trade. The hospital relies on the townspeople for performing specific maintenance problems, and the sheet metal shop, town electrician, town plumber, and town mechanic perform such services. The hospital also has its own kitchen, garage, emergency power plant, water well, and laundry. The people employed in these jobs are also semi-permanent; no job opportunity exists there for the drop-outs.

There has been a great outcry from the oil company combine, that the proposed pipeline, which would destroy Alaska's environmental integrity, is needed in order to make jobs available for the native people. Anyone who knows Alaska knows that native work for the oil companies' pipeline is nothing more than a pipe dream. The temporary jobs, low paying jobs, hard labor jobs, will go to the native people. Such jobs are good for a few years, and no hope exists again for job security and a chance to make a livelihood and raise a family. We native people know from experience that this is so.

Perhaps the greatest reason for dropping out of school is the seasonal job, which is a Nome by-product of its historic past. Ever since the birth of Nome as a white town in the early 1900's, summertime has been the most productive employment season of the year. Most of the gold mining was done during the peak periods of May through August, with September and the rest of the year seeing a shut-down of machinery and clean-up operations taking place. Such "clean-up" deals with security guards, when the gold and related minerals are collected and melted to ingots. This operation gave the most trustworthy workers the security of a winter job. In summer, the supply ships are anchored a couple of miles out in the Bering Sea, so that tenders with barges take the year's supplies to business warehouses. When this all important supply is dumped on the shores of Nome, the town is transformed from a 70 percent unemployment town, to a 30 percent unemployment town. This means that 40 percent of Nome's labor force has risen from its hangover and gone to work. Business has begun a jubilant season. There is even a shortage of manpower for skilled labor, and many outsiders come in to operate the heavy equipment.

Just before school ends, the jobs sprout up. Those same teenagers who have not been able to afford a fishing rod, rifle, or Honda, are enticed by available work. Some are able to land a job as a heavy duty machine operator and make enough money to buy whatever they have been wishing for. Like many boys in the "Lower-Forty-Eight" who lie about their ages to join the armed services, the boys in Nome often lie about their ages to work in construction jobs. When work begins, they find that what they have been taught in school is workable for people who are already established in some sort of business. The realities of life in Nome brings them the knowledge of what a construction job boss already knows. The boss, often imported, also imports with him the know-how for getting the job done. When he is finished, he takes that know-how with him. It is a vicious circle.

The potential drop-out rationalizes, if he can make a living at this work which pays him real money, without the need to learn Algebra, Shakespeare, or American History, at least for a season, he can go on to make enough to survive by job-hopping in the off-season. Unlike the migrant workers of California, or the ghetto dweller of any sizeable city, the drop-out youth of Nome is not recognized by most social workers. If he happens to be successful in his first few jobs, he is then lauded by the Nome citizenry as a good man, a hard worker; in short, one who is going to keep business alive by becoming part of the consumer class. The less fortunate ones join the class of the unemployed. They will feel too old to go back to school, where the high school kids are now hungrily grasping at the New Left's Peace ideology, the new Hard Rock, and the New Fashions. Some will consider "Relocation," a program set up by the Bureau of Indian Affairs years ago, in which natives are exported from their homes for vocational training and a promise of work elsewhere. They are thinking that nothing could be worse than living in Nome as an Eskimo. But they know that many who have gone on the Relocation program while it was the

BIA's pet project, have long since returned home, because living in a city as a dishwasher or laborer does not change his chances.

If nothing is done to correct this strange way of life, in which the Nome Eskimos are quietly suffering the effects of seasonal jobs, the welfare system, the bureaucracy of the Bureau of Indian Affairs, and the apartheid-like situation which prevails in the business atmosphere of Nome, there will be an uprising such as the Indian Wars of the West, in the 1800's. A few differences: There will be no flintlock single-shot firearms, no place to hide and run away to in the winter, and really no strong outposts to police the potential rebels who are all good shots and can make use of the weather conditions better than anyone else can. There is the rapidly growing birth rate, which is also quietly crowding the Nome Eskimo homes, as small as they are. More of these children are growing up to dare the people who are often as uneducated as their parents, but own the established Nome businesses in spite of their ignorance.

Another point to ponder: The Alaska National Guard of Northwest Alaska is made up mostly of Eskimos who are now content to train annually, usually at Ft. Richardson near Anchorage, making the best of the opportunity to travel, and a chance to unwind at the dirty, smelly bars of downtown Anchorage. If the Alaska National Guard is called in to quiet an uprising in Nome, whom would they obey?

This is not an impossible prediction of things to come, from what is commonly known as the "Last Frontier," a romantic name for an unromantic state of affairs. There are people in responsible offices of State and Federal agencies who promise, over and over again, that there will be changes made for the better, "in due time." Again we ask: Give or Take a Century — when is "due time?"

Throughout the history of Alaska, the seesaw has been between the monied investors and the natural resources, with the Alaskan natives as the uncomplaining fulcrum. The fulcrum cannot move to the money side, because it has already been predetermined that the laws he must obey call for money first before he can make money. It calls for education, but this takes money, too. If he opts for the natural resources, claiming by aboriginal rights a portion of what has been taken out by Alaska, and what will be exploited soon, the government of the United States together with the immigrant Alaska state government, will let loose with a pack of legal wolves to keep the hapless fulcrum at the center.

There are a few individuals from the wolf pack who have come to realize that the Alaskan natives are not objects to kick around, as if they were half-grown litter on the verge of self sufficiency. One such man is Justice Arthur Goldberg, chief counsel for the Alaska Federation of Natives, an organization formed by the scattered villages and communities of Northwest Alaska and the ethnically separated Eskimos, Aleuts and Indians. Justice Goldberg volunteered his services without a fee; and for his efforts, he and his partner, former Attorney General Ramsey Clark, with former Senator Thomas Kuchel, have been insulted as "outsiders . . . easterners," and other derogatory phrases.

Adequate and accurate information and intensive inter-communication is the greatest need of the Alaskan Native today. Only one newspaper in the state attempts to serve this purpose: The Tundra Times. The greatest strength of this struggling newspaper is also its unfortunate weakness. While its purpose is to inform the Native people, it does not reach them effectively. This weekly newspaper was started on October 1, 1961, after one Dr. Henry S. Forbes of Milton, Massachusetts, had been to Alaska on a fact-finding trip in 1961. He gambled on the strength of Mr. Howard Rock, the present editor and president of the "Eskimo, Indian, Aleut Publishing Co., Inc." The paper is published out of Fairbanks, Alaska. Dr. Forbes died August 15, 1968. If this newspaper fails to reach the natives which it is attempting to serve, it will leave the field open to white supremacists to do whatever they wish in the state. Misinformation, misinterpretation and misconception will continue to pass for "news" and the native people will continue to be fooled.

The schools which the native children attend are silent about the original cultures of the Eskimo, Indian and Aleut. More often they teach the young Eskimo students that a "primitive" race still exists somewhere in the Northernmost parts of the northern hemisphere, and that this race eats raw meat and lives in ice igloos. When I read this in a sixth grade geography book, it did not hit me as a piece of gross misinformation at the time. I thought this referred to some unknown primitive races still roaming around on the tip of Pt. Barrow or thereabouts 700 miles north of Nome. I hadn't the faintest idea they were talking about me. Later, when I found that the Pt. Barrow Eskimos are much more active in the village councils than many other native groups further south, I still could not believe that the school books were a source of misinformation. So I surmised that there must be igloo builders and raw meat eaters who traded wives, in the northernmost parts of Canada.

Now, with deep apologies to the Canadian Eskimo, I must alter these ideas, since they are making considerable inroads in bettering their situation, and I recognize the fact that even I was intensively brainwashed by misinformation. The schoolbook description of the Greenland Eskimos is also filled with falsification. Textbooks and other media which have been pushed at American children for the past couple of centuries is part of what is wrong in Alaska today.

Without a doubt there is prejudice against the natives in Alaska today. Prejudice, borne by the winds of the dominant class structure, fed by misinformation that passes for education, and fostered by those who want the status quo. Willie doesn't know why there should be such a thing as racism. I don't know either, why there is such a thing. I only know that the racist seeks exotic or isolated "proof" as the reason to deceive himself into thinking that another race is less qualified to be human.

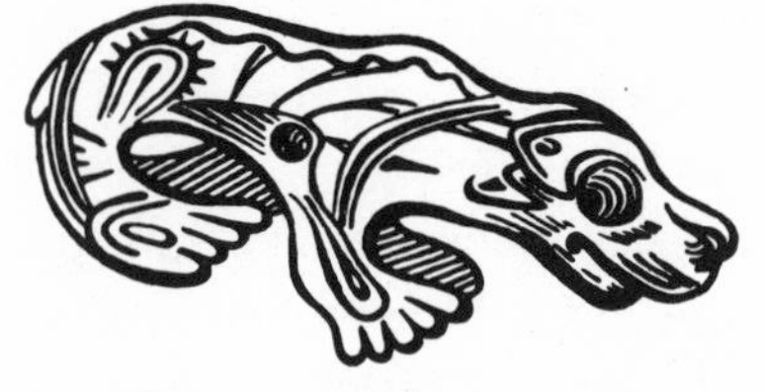

17

The Old and the New

Seals, walrus, reindeer and other animals once furnished the Eskimo with both meat and clothing. With the advent of manufactured clothing, this is no longer so. Sears Roebuck, and the other mail order companies probably do not realize how much they affected the old Eskimo way of life. If the Eskimo culture as a whole was allowed to more fairly inter-culturate with the white race, there might have been some very unique business establishments in Northwest Alaska today.

For instance, instead of killing the walrus mainly for its tusks, after some of the villages located near its migratory routes have caught enough for their subsistence, a few walrus hide tanning companies might have had a nice enterprise. Instead, those who still sew articles from hides of walrus, seal and other animals, must rely on tanning companies in the states of Washington, California, and elsewhere, since no local company tans the ultra-heavy walrus hide. After moving to Nome, my mother and father had to send the seal hides thousands of miles away — and still do. Sometimes they get the hides back in such poor condition that they can't make Eskimo boots or parkas out of them. This is because they now have little time to do their own tanning. The tanning companies don't specialize in Alaskan sea mammals. Those who still own skinboats, as my father does, find it more and more difficult to obtain walrus hides for the boats.

It now costs more than a hundred dollars for a split walrus hide in its raw state; and it has yet to be sewn together for the boat.

Many poor Nome Eskimos just leave their skinboat frames lay around to rot, because they cannot afford to replace the old and worn coverings. Last year, my father re-covered his skinboat at a high cost, and then due to his short vacation time, the early breakup of the shore ice, the lack of available help, and just plain loss of a cultural way of life, he could not set it out for a skinboat hunt. He immediately resigned from even taking a short trip with it, and covered it with tarpaulin to protect it from the elements. He hopes it will survive the rains and snows so that he may have the opportunity next year. A poignant reminder that he is a man of few remorseful feelings. He admires my White brother-in-law for his respect for things such as Eskimo foods. But he does not boast of his son-in-law's human traits, and his lack of racial prejudice.

Because of this lack of strong feeling against what he sees as a dominant culture, my father is one of many elder Eskimos in Alaska who will not jump into the hustle and bustle of modern society's aches and pains. Also, Nome being a relatively isolated Eskimo community, it offers little comparison for the "Great Society," its gains and setbacks, as opposed to the Eskimo way of life as he knows it. Only when and if an Eskimo leaves Nome or his village for other places such as Fairbanks, Anchorage, or the Lower-Forty-Eight can he compare the differences in cultures. Then, if the person has left Alaska with the preconceived idea that White society is somehow superior to the Eskimo culture, as can be expected from the type of education which American Natives receive, he is generally a very disillusioned individual. This disillusionment is something my father has not cared to analyze. He has his own personal philosophy: To do as much as he can to provide for his family; to try and enjoy some of the things which he grew up with; and to leave it up to the sons and daughters, as to whether they want to retain their ancestors' heritage, or wish to progress in another way.

Predictably, this has produced a family with varying degrees of concern for the worth of Eskimo culture. Nome life in the 1950's, the 1960's, and now the 1970's, has taken its devastating toll of the Native culture. But then, during the 1880's and thereafter, Eskimo culture in its various areas began and continued to incur cultural shocks of varying degrees. Today there is still an identifiable Eskimo culture even if slightly "folded, spindled, or mutilated."

There are many Eskimos in Nome today who espouse the same sort of determined patriotism which my father has chosen as his model for showing his children the reasons for hope. Unfortunately, when or if the children decide that his model or example, or his patriotism is too dry and empty, too unproductive for them; or if there is the least bit of doubt, they are very apt to try the last thing they would want to do to their earnest, hard working parents: revolt. Rebel. In looking back, this sort of rebellion seems to me almost as dry and empty as the reason to rebel in the first place. For sure, it builds up a lot of mixed-up emotions within the immediate family, but it does not go as far as a second or third generation Eskimo would at first expect. He is not disowned by his parents, and he does not all of a sudden fall into the pit of hell and damnation. He becomes bitter, but he does not or cannot go any further. That is, he will not pursue the issue any further. Father and son just stop talking to each other. This is probably much the same as the so-called "generation gap" worrying so many White middle class families today. Perhaps some possibility exists of minimizing the immediate family priorities and concentrating on the "Family of Man."

Just a few centuries ago, the Eskimo's main concerns were those for his own family and his immediate fellow villagers. Now those values are brutally cast aside. It shows in the lack of concern for the Eskimo culture in the school books. It shows in the living standards of many Eskimos in Northwestern Alaska. It will produce some of the most devastating rebellion to rock the peaceful tundra since the withdrawal of the last glacial period. And this rebellion will not be merely within family groups, once the general feeling of younger Eskimos turns from the meek, inactive acceptance of a dominant culture's say-so. It is bound to turn to active participation in the growing Native American movements.

The young people of Alaska are in desperate need of direction. Some sort of a beginning, or reference point. Hopefully, this book may be read and digested by them, and can be used as one of many other books to indicate that very important first step. If it is not so terribly exciting now, to be part of the most Northwestern area of the United States, tomorrow may prove to be a time when an Alaskan Eskimo can say with pride that he originates from one of the most exciting places in the world. Not because it is "the land where the sun never sets in the summer," but because it is "a land where poverty, welfarism and bureaucracy have finally disappeared over the horizon," due to the re-awakening of the original inhabitants.

As far as my own generation is concerned, it really has been an interesting mixture of the old and the new. Not "the old and the new" in the popular sense, but in the sense of "the old" being the past of a little known culture yet having the ability to say that my birthplace still retains much of its cultural affinities. And then, to know that "the new" is comprised of such things as the recent oil discovery which is threatening to upset the state's ecology and economy by its very size, or the testing of the will and power of the United States Congress, by the small in size but large in will power, Alaska Federation of Natives.

The real problem today is that there is little time to ponder the question of whether to get involved in such things as Native Rights, Civil Rights, or Native Leadership. Time is moving, getting shorter and shorter for those of us who would pause a moment to ponder our "self-involvement." There are just too many people who are not Alaskan Natives, who are willing to exploit as much labor, natural resources, and cultural uniqueness out of the Alaskan Natives as they can.

Education remains the greatest barrier to Native progress. Usually the Nome Eskimos from the ages of about 40 on, have only a partial grade school education. My father completed the seventh grade, but went no further. My mother probably completed the fourth grade. Of those under 40, there are a few who have gone past the eighth grade, usually those who were fortunate enough to attend a regional high school or a parochial school away from their home village. Some have even gone to places like the Haskell Indian Institute in Kansas, Chilocco in Oklahoma, and later to the University of Alaska. However, even for many in their 30's, any education past high school is rare indeed. In my family, my oldest brother is in his late 30's. He has a BFA degree. My oldest sister finished high school. My second older brother completed three years of college. My younger sister dropped out of school in her freshman high school year. I have recently received my BFA degree. Our family has been fortunate in having had so many school years completed by its members. The fact is that there are very few Eskimo families that have had the opportunity for complete schooling for all or even for most of its members. It will be interesting to see how many of the grandchildren of Willie Senungetuk will attain the one thing which he himself could only hope for his children: a good education.

The grandchildren of Willie are as varied and unique as the times in which they were born. My oldest sister has a son and a daughter. My oldest brother has a son and daughter. My second older brother married an Eskimo from the Teller area. They have five children. My younger sister has three daughters. My wife Jan and I have a little daughter, Jennifer. Some of these grandchildren of Willie's are "half-breeds." This term, I realize, is a vulgarization; but it is a term I grew up with, complete with its Eskimo-ized corruption, "Hoff breekh." There is also an Eskimo term used for illegitimate children, "Opp pay lik," which means "without father."

When my wife and I went up to Nome a summer ago, my nephew asked if we could send him a "peace symbol brooch." Probably this is an indication of the concern of our Eskimo youth with the unpopular war in Asia, which has created a sense of unity with the youth of the Lower-Forty-Eight. Indeed the distance and isolation of many villages from so-called "civilized" areas are lessened a great deal for our young people today, largely through the mass media. There is also a saddening thought about the resulting introduction of strobe lights and electric guitars in the interests of our young. These desires of the young Eskimos and mixed-bloods to sample the cultural fads of the White man are a symptom of their anxiety to be "with it." It would be a much better transitional approach for both the Natives and the non-

Natives of Alaska if the youth were made to feel at least comfortable with their parents' cultural standards. Instead, the children of the villages find it difficult to accept the fact that mukluks and parkas are much warmer and more sensible to wear in Northwest Alaska than mini-skirts and sandals. That the sounds of the Eskimo dance and the Eskimo drum are just as exciting and moving (if not more so), as the throbs and twangs of the electric guitar. That there is no "face" to lose if one were to help the parents when they are out hunting or fishing, or doing other things in "the Eskimo way."

Also, there is great advantage in combining the Eskimo culture with the white culture so far as mode of dress, entertainment, and many other activities. There are some young Nomites who are doing exactly this. A good example is the group my wife and I saw when we went to Nome to instruct interested members of the Sunarit Associates, in printmaking. This is an Eskimo cooperative which makes ivory and soapstone carvings, slippers and other forms of arts and crafts for sale to tourists and collectors. As it turned out, the older Sunarit members were not interested in expanding their production, or improving their arts to reach a more sophisticated market. On the other hand, the young people of King Island Village revealed great interest in learning a new form of art. For three weeks, they had a wonderful time, and produced a great amount of work. I myself was highly gratified to see how the short-time program evolved and progressed, and to understand why the young people were so eager and the older ones so reluctant.

The age group showing most interest was that from ten years to seventeen. This group, especially the younger ten to twelve year olds, were bilingual. Since I had been away from Nome for about ten years, they did not know me. Therefore they would attempt to use their knowledge of the Eskimo language to keep themselves from being understood while talking of personal matters. My theory, to explain their ability to speak Eskimo so fluently, is that their parents and their peers are still close together and they have a better chance to retain the language. There are more opportunities to talk together. Other Eskimo families, whose children have lost their language, have not been capable of remaining a cohesive family group. In many ways, the King Island Village can be compared with the ghetto areas of any large city in the Lower-Forty-Eight. Yet it is an area of Nome which includes a mere three or four city blocks. There are probably about thirty families directly involved in the Nome-King Island Village proper, with a probable average of six members per family. They came to find jobs, and education for their children. Some could not find jobs, so they became fairly well-known ivory carvers. Others have found steady jobs wherever they could. A few work for the Nome Hospital, some work for the Bureau of Public Roads; some at grocery and general merchandise stores.

In the early 1960's, two or three families had earned enough to afford their own homes, or to rent houses, so they could move away from the "East End" of Nome. Another two or three could afford to repair their homes, add additions or make improvements. They chose to remain in the East End. Now there are a few attractive homes there. Later, however, some few families did move to other areas: Anchorage or Fairbanks. The types of housing in the East End of Nome are just as varied as the types of jobs which the largely uneducated villagers have attained. Possibly the poorest houses are the post-Second World War army huts which were bought after the Nome army camp was dissolved. A row of four or five of these metal and masonite scrap-heaps line the back of East End, atop the soggy tundra. Others are rickety frame houses with electrical wiring installed thirty years ago. The newer and better built frame houses are few in number and it is a never-ending chore of maintenance to keep up with the caprices of the perma-frost. To build larger houses would incur larger heating bills. So the Nome villagers usually choose cramped quarters rather than spend needed food and clothing money on stove oil.

In the crowded, dilapidated structures, the children's lives are cramped in every way. In school, most teachers have no knowledge of the children's state of mind, except to be vaguely aware of the existing poverty. I myself did not know just what to expect of the teenagers in my printmaking class. To be sure, there were things I allowed in class that would have been absolute prohibitions by their schoolteachers. Young boys, as young as seven or eight years, as soon as they learned I would not object to their strange little customs, pulled out their Copenhagen snuff boxes from their pockets with pride and a show of manliness. They offered me some, and I did take a little from one small boy who was very excited about the printmaking project. Generally, one of the things that all small boys do is to imitate their fathers and older brothers. And one of the things that King Island Village men do, is chew snuff. For one thing, it is much cheaper than cigarettes or pipe tobacco. For another, it was one of the items that the early traders and whalers brought along to Alaska to trade for furs and ivory. The villagers naturally learned to enjoy chewing snuff. During hunting trips, chewing tobacco is simpler than to smoke cigarettes or a pipe. It is not hindered by strong winds, salt water, or strenuous physical activity. So it is not surprising to me that the little boys would have an affinity for the little red and black round can.

The girls grouped themselves into small circles. A couple of them produced some nice prints, despite the fact that they had to tolerate the scorn of some of the boys, who felt that the girls' interests should be more in sewing and housekeeping. So it went, for three short weeks, in which I realized that this project smacked of some of the familiar "make-work" projects, which really do not accomplish much. Nevertheless, I feel that it can open up some new direction in the methods of teaching young Eskimos in places like Nome.

One of the questions dealing with developing Northwest Alaska is connected with the land. Who owns the land? Who should benefit directly or indirectly from the sales, leases, and ownership of the land? Who should have control over decisions about the land?

The one different element from the old story of who is to derive money and benefits from the land, ownership of which is a matter of dispute between the original owners and the encroaching immigrants, is that the Northwest Alaskan Natives and the rest of the country's Native Americans are now wise to governmental deception. The Alaska Federation of Natives is asking for very reasonable compensation for lands taken by State and Federal governments. Negotiations so far between the Native organization and the United States Government have yielded only the smallest concessions from the government, concessions that are unacceptable to the Natives of Alaska.

Today the Alaskan Natives are still trying to keep this country from making the same mistakes it has made from its beginnings. The government so far has refused to acknowledge the rights and claims of the remaining natives. The struggle goes on, and it must end in victory for the Natives . . . but one may ask, at what cost? As in most cases involving the federal and state relationship with the original peoples of this land, by the time agreements are reached, most of the oldtimers are dead, or funds have been expended in the struggle to such an extent that the victory is an empty one.

Alaska has paid for itself many times over. The original amount paid by the United States to Russia has yielded massive profits: in gold, land, business, and the use of natural resources. But misconceptions and misinformation still continue about the rights of the Natives. Who do you turn to for correction of popular misconceptions? The educational system? The legal system? Or are those systems in themselves part of a larger misconception. I am sure that some of the Native leaders in Alaska are at the point where they are asking themselves these questions. If they and the institutions they are appealing to do not come up with some good answers, then in another century, another time, we shall find more injustices which will in turn create more racial tensions, more impoverishment, and such massive internal dissent as could very well tear this nation apart.

18

The Hide Box

It is like an unreal dream to return to Nome from anywhere in the Lower-Forty-Eight. From either stopover, Fairbanks or Anchorage, the last leg of the jet ride takes a couple of hours over a vast expanse of mountains and lowlands. It is like watching everything running backwards like a clock or an old movie going in reverse. Each landing place is like subtracting everything that makes up middle American towns and cities a little bit more. Like erasing a picture on a blackboard a little at a time. First, the multi-storied buildings and the elaborate air terminals rub off. Then the freeways and the fast traffic. Then the edges of the cities. (You draw in some mountains and rivers.) A landing at Anchorage or Fairbanks; there are still trees on the fringes of the city. Then you erase more of the larger buildings and more of the roads. Erase the air terminal, and draw in a gray old Army hangar for the landing at Nome.

There are no trees. Only some taling piles from the now dead gold dredges. One would have to erase the whole blackboard and draw in a completely different picture to depict the landing at Wales. It is almost impossible to imagine the sights, the really open land. In a way, he who has travelled a long way from home is fortunate. But he does not realize it if he boasts of his "big city" experiences to the less travelled villagers. Such boasting only fortifies the position of the non-native Alaskan that Alaska should discard all Native values in exchange for so-called "development". Such as smog, traffic congestion, commercials, neon signs, drugs, the dog-eat-dog ideology, environmental pollution, or nervous indigestion? What such a person should dig is his own background, before he can enjoy the other things. Then perhaps Nome would have something better to offer his children than what he has had.

Racism in Nome is quite different than that known in the Lower-Forty-Eight. There is a more subtle form of prejudice, which becomes apparent to those who remain in Nome longer than a few months. This is the usual length of stay for imported construction workers during the summer. Tourists, construction laborers, and occasional itinerant employees are strangers to the profoundly alienated feelings between the "friendly, always smiling" Eskimos and the "hard working, earnest" Whites of Nome. The Eskimos are indeed friendly. They do not feel offended even if they are discriminated against. The Nome schools were segregated as late as 1945. During 1950-59, as a student in the Nome public schools, I was beaten by half-breed boys for being an Eskimo, and personally witnessed the discrimination against the King Island Eskimo children. The White students generally kept to themselves, as though to make believe we didn't even exist. The Native children gathered in their own village groups. I believe this is true even today. The latest village group now being taunted by both white students and natives of other villages is the St. Lawrence Islander, who recently started moving to Nome in families, after some of their men had come to Nome for seasonal jobs and National Guard duty. Thus, discrimination and prejudice exist not only between Whites and Eskimos, but also between Eskimos of one village and those of another, although to a lesser extent in the latter case.

Certain subtleties are these: Eskimo drunks are incarcerated at any time they become intoxicated, while Whites are ignored in this condition, even if the evidence against the Whites surpasses that against the Natives. If some attempt at equal justice is made by new police officials, they are generally ousted out of their jobs. Credit is not extended to Natives unless they are subjected to the most outrageous investigation both of a personal and business nature. On the other hand, the city of Nome has been victimized by outsiders, who have defrauded the townspeople as well as the business community. During the later 1950's, a couple opened a store, obtaining easy credit from many businessmen in Nome. Three years later, they left the town for "a buying trip." They never returned to Nome, leaving unpaid bills and many creditors foaming at the mouth. During the next ten years, Nome hired a city manager. He came in like a bolt of lightning, spending money freely and moving in and out of the town on business trips which taxed the city's finances needlessly. He was fired some months later with a full year's pay.

Until just a few years ago, seating arrangements in the churches were such that the Eskimo sat in one section and the white churchgoers in another. The city council has always been run by white businessmen. The Nome Nugget, the town's only newspaper, has a weekly drunk list that consists only of Eskimos. There are many more such subtleties of rank prejudice, discrimination, attitudes which deny the Natives the slightest respect. It is all regarded by Nome generally (and also by my father), as a generally acceptable state of affairs. He knew that the price to be paid for his decision to move to Nome would involve acceptance of such situations.

Dad has always regarded the White man as part of a very clever race of people. Radios, airplanes, automobiles, gold dredges, ships, rifles, outboard motors, clocks and watches, writing pens, tractors, and many other non-Eskimo items never fail to elicit from him his wonder and delight: "How clever these White men," he would observe.

In November, 1969, the Eskimo was made a matter of international study, not in the United States, but in a special conference held in Paris, France. This was a meeting of specialists, scientists, and representatives of the Eskimo population from Alaska, Greenland, and Canada, with official representatives from the nations of Canada, Denmark and Russia. The subject was "the Arctic Development and the Future of the Eskimo societies." The United States did not send a representative. But a bright young Eskimo from Kotzebue, Alaska, came to the meeting to explain the current situation, the conditions, and the possibilities for the future of his fellow Eskimos. William L. Hensley spoke to a distinguished, world-renowned group of men and women. He gave a scholarly overview of the current situation in Alaska, well worth incorporating here, in part:

> "America will lose an opportunity to right old wrongs," said Hensley, "and for once to allow the First Americans a fair deal, if there is no settlement, or a poor settlement of the Native land claims issue. We know the history of our country in dealing with the American Indian and we want to see the final chapter not written in blood or injustice. If the final chapter in this history reveals a just settlement of the issue, the Natives will be able to live longer and more decently, without having to stoop in indignity because of a degrading welfare system, and the young natives will be able to seek education and new opportunities. If there is no settlement or a poor one, relations between Natives and Whites may be marred for years. It may bring defeatism to the people and will prevent us from becoming an integral part of Alaska's social and economic development."

Explaining the historic background of the present situation, Mr. Hensley's words may be paraphrased for the sake of brevity, as follows:

Without consulting with the Natives, the Russian government sold Alaska in 1867 to the United States. At that time there were approximately 35,000 Natives and only 400 White people in the Territory. The protection of Native rights to lands actually in their use or occupation was provided for in the Organic Act of 1884. When Alaska became a state in 1959, its constitution stated that the State and its people disclaim all rights or title to any property which is claimed by a Native. However, the matter was not settled then. Conflicts arose when Congress authorized the new state to select 103 million acres from the land mass of Alaska . . . land that was being used and occupied by the Native villagers. To serve as a statewide vehicle through which the Natives could work for a settlement, the Alaska Federation of Natives was formed, and 30 percent of the voting public — the Natives — became a unified force. The Federation's first course of action was to work for a halt to the disposition of land to the State, until Congress could make a determination regarding Native claims.

Such a halt, Mr. Hensley explained, known as the "Land Freeze," was soon instituted by the Secretary of the Interior, thus withdrawing all Alaskan lands from disposal until Congress could act. However, if Congress takes no action, the "freeze" will be lifted. The Natives have gone this route rather than proceeding through the courts, because a court settlement would be a costly and lengthy route, and would result in no land grants, and small money payments. Under the Statehood Act, Congress retained absolute jurisdiction over the disposition of the Native land claims issue. Only Congress can confirm or extinguish Native ownership.

"In making its decision," Hensley continued, "The legislative body will shape the future of Eskimo generations to come, and the relationship of these generations to the White man."

People tend to speak of Alaska as a "young, growing, naive, fresh, virgin, rugged, adventuresome state. If these descriptions mean that Alaska is short on sophistication and finesse, and the rest of the United States has attained the accolade of stately maturity, how can my old man's father's father's old man have attained anything resembling good taste and skill, when he hadn't even the opportunity to meet those who so wisely "discovered" the New World? Like, I mean, it has become some sort of an aristocratic privilege to be admitted to the United States. It took Alaska years to convince the aged Congressmen that there were some redeeming qualities in the land and its people. To belong to the Union, it takes taxing ourselves practically out of existence as individual human beings with normal needs, desires, and rights. But money is King in democractic America, and programs as well as proposals are tied to money instead of to human values and needs.

Altogether different values exist among those peoples who once belonged to an entirely different system, the Natives of this land who were so unlike the money-minded oppressed of other times and places such as the European Jews.

A person was worth his sweat in terms of directly fulfilling the human need of providing life to life. Religion also bore a part, as a direct relationship of Man to his Maker, his own superior being asking for benevolence, when and if anyone seemed to act against nature. Health resolved itself by reinforcing those who worked the hardest physically and mentally. Welfare, in the form of *help* for others was a rule of life, so that too much dependence upon others immediately opened a safety valve, while all the other social balances were obvious and easily felt. Wealth was felt simply and collectively by appraising one's tools for adding to the security of the family and the land, as far as the eye could see. Measurement was in tune with the feeling one had with the whole universe, be it as tiny as an atom, or as large as the cosmos. Even if there was a challenge to admit to one's fraility, one had the secure insight of being comfortable with the most complex of all chemical complexes — the self.

There is an analogy I could make in connection with the attitudes and actions of the dominant White society towards the Natives of Alaska. We have, among our people, an article of utility called a "Hide Box." It was constructed of walrus hide, the full thickness, and was used to store treasured personal possessions. It was molded when the skin was still wet, formed into a box approximately 18 inches by 13, and was generally decorated with one-dimensional drawings of mythical birds and animals. This small item of utility was much prized by the ancient ones, and is today practically non-existent due to the use of wood and nails.

And so the Hide Box has become a sort of curiosity, much loved by the Native people, still utilized for personal possessions by those fortunate enough to have one. In its small, restricted place there has rested a great deal of memorabilia, but we have never placed a human being there, either physically or in spirit, or even in thought.

Today our life can be described as one of existence in the restricting framework of an alien civilization, an alien Hide Box. Through the government itself and its agencies; through the complete lack of understanding of our culture and history; through the mouths of the teachers and lecturers and statesmen who speak for America — we are crushed in a Hide Box. The foreigners who have painted the Hide Box with representations of the Native cultures as savage, useful only as excuses for take-over of valuable

Native land, requiring "christianizing" to make us more pliable, have done this. The Hide Box, as used by the aliens who came among us, has become the embodiment of isolation. Isolation of the Natives while strangers took his land. And the Natives still ask: What could perfect strangers possibly do with all this land? Europeans had already become hardened to the effects of a new technological age when they came to our land. The value system of this technological age is that profits come first and Man comes next. But the Eskimos and the American Indians might have gone through eons of perfecting their involvement with nature, before electing to switch to easier modes of living, without loss of integrity either of the land or of Mankind.

Today the voice of the Native in the Hide Box is heard echoing within its thinning walls. Pushed further and further westward, it now contains Man, still proud, who cannot be contained much longer. The hide is losing its shape and strength. Its contents are responding to these changes. The original mythical designs have long lost their meaning to the onlooker, who thought the figures were made only for sale to tourists.

We Eskimos have given centuries of our lives and history to the European alien, give or take a few. The aliens who came among us have taken and taken, and still it does not end. Alaska today is like a walrus sitting on the visible part of an iceberg, grunting slogans of provincial patriotism, refusing to recognize the massive three-quarters of submerged and moving ice. Submerged though the Native may be today, his strength is mounting, his knowledge growing, and his will to change the future of his children is not any longer to be ignored.

Chronology: Alaska Native History

It is believed that Alaska's earliest people, the Natives of the land, came to the area approximately 10,000 to 20,000 B.C. They discovered and settled various regions of Alaska and Canada. The Eskimo people are known to have settled as far as Greenland. Only the oral literature of the Natives can tell the story of their earliest life. There is no written history. Anthropologists and archaeologists have, however, been able to reconstruct certain parts of the life of the Natives, and some clue as to the early Eskimos is offered, in the words of Swanton and Henshaw, published in the *Handbook of American Indians North of Mexico* (F.W. Hodge, ed., Bureau of American Ethnology, Bulletin #30):

"There has always been intertribal communication. The Eskimo have an exceptional knowledge of the geography of their country. Poetry and music play an important part in their life, especially in connection with their religious observances." (Vol. 1, p. 434.)

"They are peculiar as being the only race of American Aborigines who certainly had contact with white people before the days of Columbus, for Greenland was occupied during the 10th and 11th centuries by Norwegians, whose expeditions extended even as far as the American mainland . . . The Eskimos have proved almost indispensable assistants to Arctic explorers." (Vol. 1, p. 435.)

Dr. Margaret Lantis, in a paper read to the Second Inter-American Conference on Indian Life, at Cuzco, Peru, in 1949 said:

"Settlers, including members of the Armed Services, entering north and west Alaska, need the Eskimo's amazing knowledge of the region. Outsiders must depend upon the Eskimo's work, using his special ability to subsist in the rigorous environment, his skills, initiative and self-sufficiency. In addition, the newcomers must learn to live like him, learning from Eskimos the special problems and resources of hunting, food, clothing, transportation, heating, in the Arctic and sub-Arctic."

What has been said in *Give or Take a Century* by its Eskimo author, and what is now emphasized, perhaps needlessly, is that the Eskimo people had a complex, satisfying, technologically developed culture prior to white contact. As an interesting possibility for a future study of the Eskimo people, this Chronology in Native Alaska History is presented. As stated before, no specific dates may be given for the history of the Native peoples before contact with the Europeans. Indeed this is true of many civilizations. It is true of the literature of the Bible, as another example, which was written long after the events presumed to have occurred.

Perhaps one of the more reliable ways of understanding the history of the Native peoples, however, is through their arts and inventions. Studying their arts, one may begin to understand the heart and spirit of a people. Examining their inventions, one may reconstruct the long and arduous road which they have traveled, their experiments and vicissitudes, their magnificent march through thousands of years of discovery and settlement. In the knowledge obtained from this kind of study, one may acquire some small inkling of the magnitude of their progress in time and place. A small beginning in this type of study is made, following the Chronology, in the list of inventions and contributions made by the Native peoples of Alaska to the people of North America and indeed to the world as a whole, which is offered as part of this book.

Following contact with the Europeans, the Natives experienced a cataclysmic change in their way of life. It is fitting, therefore, that this Chronology begin with the first of such contacts.

1741: Western Alaska Natives' first look at Europeans, when Vitus Bering and Alexei Chirikof make contact with the Alaska coast and islands.

1741-1867: This was the era of confrontation between the Native peoples and the foreigners. Russia sends expeditions to Alaska and the Aleutian Islands, places the Aleuts in feudal bondage, leading to virtual extermination of the people. The Tlingits revolt time and again, and resistance is felt during the entire period, from the Aleuts as well as the other Natives.

September, 1762: Natives of the Aleutian Islands revolt against the Russians, forcing the recall of Russian detachments. Aleuts protest outrages upon 14 Aleut girls who were commanded by one Sgt. Pushkaref to gather food for his ship's company. The girls were put on board a ship, raped and beaten. One was murdered. Twelve committed suicide by throwing themselves into the sea. (H. H. Bancroft, *Alaska,* p. 1129.)

December, 1762: Aleuts retaliate for Russian butcheries. Three Russians — Drushinnin, Shekalef, and Shevyrin — are attacked. The Natives lay siege for four days to the Russian outpost, in an attempt to rid their islands of the invaders. They simultaneously attack three Russian detachments, and maintain their their attacks for five weeks, despite their ill-matched weaponry as against the Imperial Russian guns and gunpowder. The Russians were saved only by their advanced weaponry and an ample supply of gunpowder. According to Bancroft, "A majority of all the Natives . . . paid with their lives for presuming to defend their homes against invaders, (page 51). One Russian, Soloviev, was said to have murdered as many as 3,000 Aleuts, blowing up homes with gunpowder and executing Natives en masse." (Ibid.)

1764: Aleuts finally submit to Russian invasion. From then on, they are used as forced labor, placed in feudal slavery, and form the work force for the Russian fur industry. Resistance continues, but in an ever diminishing degree, as the Aleuts are murdered or die of disease and hard labor.

July, 1766: Aleut submission is complete. Natives of the important Aleutian Islands are finally overpowered. The population decreases by 70 percent. Tribute is exacted from them by the Russians until 1779.

1763-1766: Natives on Unmak and Unalaska Islands resist. They destroy a Russian boat, and conflict grows between these Natives and the Russian invaders.

August 24, 1776: The Natives on Prince of Wales Island in southeastern Alaska get their first view of the Spanish invader. Juan Francisco de la Bodega Y Cuadra arrives on the west coast of the islands, landing on Forrester Island. He is met by a vacant sea and empty land.

1783: The furs and hunting grounds of the Aleutian Islands are ravaged, leaving a land of waste, and an economic desert for the Aleutians. Invaders turn their attention to the mainland.

1783-1784: Kodiak, Cook Inlet, and the Chugaches Natives resist invasion.

1783-1787: This was the era of organized Tlingit revolt, creating havoc among the Russian invaders. Fighting with bows and arrows, slingshots, and makeshift weapons, the Tlingits resisted for years, creating a history of militancy and courage which was to become part of the Tlingit tradition.

June 19, 1796: Eleven boys and "several grown men" attend missionary school at Kodiak. The priest read the prayers, and on the following day, when school was closed, the students were put to work at fishing. Father Juvenal reported they "caught 103 salmon of large size." During these years, Catholic missions were opened on the islands and mainland of Alaska.

June 24, 1802: The Natives of Sitka plan and execute an attack against the Russian interlopers. They successfully repel the Russian force at Sitka, and destroy their fort.

1805: Tlingits of Sitka are forced to make a treaty with the Russians.

June 7, 1818: Natives on the northwest side of Prince of Wales Island resist an invasion by Roquefeuil, a merchant of Bordeaux, France, who arrived on the ship *Bordelais*. He is forced to move his vessel away from their shores. On June 17, the Natives defend themselves against another attempt by the French to invade their land.

April 17, 1823: A Russian-American treaty is signed, permitting the citizens of Imperial Russia and the United States to navigate and fish in the Pacific Ocean. Article IV of the treaty provides that citizens of both countries are permitted to trade with the Natives. The Eskimos, Aleuts, and the Indians have no knowledge of the treaty, nor of any of its provisions. Nor had they been consulted in the negotiations, or in the development of the events following the treaty, in which first steps were taken to divide the Alaskan resources among these great powers.

1838: Eskimos on the Alaskan coast attack a ship's company under Alexander Kashevarof, preventing a landing on their shores. The Russians are compelled to turn back.

1841-1852: During these years, the whaling industry of the foreigners grows to a peak of 14 million dollars in 278 vessels. The Native people are robbed, forced into servitude, their women raped. Sometimes a bottle of whiskey is "traded" for $200 in furs.

1867: The Natives learn to their surprise that two foreign countries, having no title to their land, nor any rights to its resources, have bought and sold their entire property. The United States buys Alaska for $7,200,000. The Natives are neither consulted nor is their permission asked. This must be the biggest land steal in history, since the State of Alaska is nearly one-fifth the entire area of the United States, and contains some of the most valuable resources in the world. The treaty of the United States with Russia, signed pursuant to the sale of the Indian-Eskimo-Aleut property, provided:

> "The inhabitants of the ceded territory (Alaska), according to their choice, reserving their natural allegiance, may return to Russia within three years; but if they should prefer to remain in the ceded territory, they, with the exception of uncivilized native tribes, shall be admitted to the enjoyment of all the rights, advantages, and immunities of citizens of the United States, and shall be maintained and protected in the free enjoyment of their liberty, property, and religion. The uncivilized tribes will be subject to such laws and regulations as the

United States may from time to time adopt in regard to the aboriginal tribes of that country."

In 1908, the courts of the United States decided upon the following test of "civilization," ". . . as to whether or not the persons in question have turned aside from old associations, former habits of life, and easier modes of existence; in other words, have exchanged the old, barbaric uncivilized environment for the one changed, new, and so different as to indicate an advanced and improved condition of mind, which desires and reaches out for something altogether distinct and unlike the old life." (P. 488, 3 Alaska, 1908.)

In the same decision, the court stated, with overbearing loftiness, that "Civilization . . . includes . . . more than a prosperous business, a trade, a house, white man's clothes, and membership in a church." (P. 491.) Not stated, but certainly implicit in current and later activities of the government and its agencies, was the accepted policy that Natives might be accorded the "benefits" of civilization if they would agree to part with their land and its resources.

In comparison, it might be mentioned that the imperial law of Russia recognized the "settled natives" (Aleuts, Kodiaks, Eskimos, Tlingits included), who embraced the Christian faith, as Russian citizens on the same footing as white subjects. But, "the independent tribes of pagan faith who acknowledged no restraint from the Russians, and practiced their ancient customs, were classed as "uncivilized native tribes." At the same time, in the charter of the Russian-American Company, a new racial designation is made, that of "creoles," who are defined as "children born of a European or Siberian father and a native American mother, or of a native American father and a European or Siberian mother, shall be regarded as creoles, equally with the children of these latter of whom a special record shall be kept."

1869: Five hundred soldiers are stationed in Alaska by the United States, remaining there until 1877, despite the protests of both the native and non-native population. The natives face infamous treatment by the United States. Sitka sustained the greatest horrors of those years of military occupation. Even such a man as William S. Dodge, U.S. collector of customs, accused the soldiers of "contaminating the natives." Rape was common; drunkenness was the rule among the military. Documented evidence proves that many cases of murder occurred, by the military against the natives, and many evidences of torture inflicted upon the natives by the Americans were revealed in later documented charges. Nevertheless, upon the final withdrawal of troops from Sitka, no retaliatory measures were taken by the Indians, although this was anticipated.

1872: The Aleuts received 40 cents for each fur seal skin delivered to the Alaska Commercial Company of America. The United States tax alone on each seal skin was $2.62.

May 17, 1884: Congress passed the *Organic Act* (23 Stat. 24). This Act made Alaska a civil and judicial district. International competition in salmon and fur industries, and growing interest in mineral resources of the territory pressured Congress for passage of the Act. It was designed to strengthen administrative control of the United States over "neglected lands." It provided for a Governor, a Judge, District Attorney, a Marshall, Clerk, and four Commissioners appointed by the President. Sitka became Alaska's first capital, and the Commissioners were stationed at Sitka, Wrangell, Juneau and Unalaska. Provisions were made, but not carried out, for the education of children "regardless of race." Sheldon Jackson introduces a missionary system of education, a proselytizing system of religious teaching and practice. From this date (1884) until March 16, 1931, a special Bureau of Education controlled both native education and welfare work. Under the Organic Act of 1884 it was decreed that the Natives were not to be disturbed in the possession of any lands actually in their use and occupancy of the land claimed by them. The Eskimos refused to ratify a proposal to establish two reservations in northern Alaska.

1890: Protestant missionaries hold conference to allot and restrict areas of native education and Christian training to the various denominations. These schools were established, mainly on the Panhandle in southeastern Alaska: 16 day schools by the government; 9 contract schools both by missionary and government; 10 mission schools, with church funds.

1891-1892: Siberian reindeer are bought and taken to Teller, (a total of 1,280 animals), designed to introduce a natural native industry.

1896-1899: Gold is discovered in various parts of Alaska, at different times, and a dozen paddlewheeled steamers and launches plied Yukon river carrying hundreds of frenzied miners and their supplies. There is no regard and little respect for native land or resources.

1898: Native villagers are left facing starvation, when a white teacher, William T. Lopp, directed a drive of 400 reindeer from Wales to Point Barrow, to save the stranded crews of eight whaling vessels. The native economy collapsed. Some Eskimos obtained seasonal jobs in local fisheries in the Bristol Bay area. Others turned to trapping foxes and muskrats.

1900: The first law enforcement officers are placed in Eskimo land, but only by request of the white gold miners in Nome. An epidemic of measles killed 25 percent of the Eskimo population. An attempt is made to correct the extremely inadequate school system, and the Nelson Act is passed by Congress, placing school management directly under the administrative control of the Governor of Alaska.

1902: The school boards of Juneau and Ketchikan refuse Indian and Eskimo student enrollment.

1903: Only two Eskimos are known to be active in the teaching profession, as assistant teachers. One in Unalakleet and one in Wales.

1904: Wales Eskimos buy reindeer business-related supplies directly from San Francisco, in order to avoid costs incurred by government-proposed middlemen.

January 27,1905: A dual educational and racist school system is set up by Congress, for the natives of Alaska. One part of the system was devoted to the white children and the other to the children of the natives. According to this law, (33 Stat. 616,619, Sec. 7), it was provided that ". . . schools for and among the Eskimos and Indians of Alaska shall be provided for by an annual appropriation, and the Eskimo and Indian children of Alaska shall have the same right to be admitted to any Indian boarding school as the Indian children in the States or Territories of the United States."

1905: Governor Gruening of Alaska reports that 20 years after the U.S. federal government had assumed responsibility for education, "at least three quarters of the Native school children were without schooling . . . Adult education . . . was particularly undreamed of."

1907: Unalakleet Eskimos independently build and man seven or eight small schooners for a shipping business in Northwest Alaska.

1910: Alaskan native reindeer herds grow to 27,325, ranging in areas from Pt. Barrow to Ugashik, from Wales to Tanana up the Yukon river.

1911: There is an enormous increase in tuberculosis and other communicable diseases among the native people, brought in with the European immigrants since the first years of white contact with the Russians in 1741, followed by the Spaniards, French and the Americans. Diseases and recurrent epidemics are unabated. Bureau of Education attached five doctors and two nurses to its payroll and subsidizes a medical missionary at Barrow, and a private physician in Nome.

1912: Alaska is made a Territory of the United States, but this has no effect upon the native peoples, who continue to live in poverty and disease.

August 24, 1912: Second Organic Act passed (c. 387, 37 Stat. 512); it provided for a civil government. The First Organic Act (1884) provided only a partial civil government.

1913: Indians, Aleuts and Eskimos suffer increased hardships, due to the depressed condition of the whaling business.

1913: Alaska Native Brotherhood is organized with the announced purpose of preparing the Natives of Alaska to exercise the rights and duties of citizenship.

1914: Natives now count a white schoolteacher, a white fur trader, and a white missionary in every Eskimo village of 100 or more population. Fur trade continues depressed, the fox population decreases. The Lomen Company, a white Nome enterprise, buys several thousand reindeer from Lapland in order to feed the company workers. This is done despite a government ruling of 1907 against white ownership of reindeer herds.

July 5, 1915: Tanana chiefs and village headmen meet at Thomas Memorial Library in Fairbanks with U.S. government officials. Members of the Athabascan tribal stock, their main requests involved education and jobs. The Tanana leaders came at their own expense. At this time, Alaska was being surveyed for a railroad. The Indians were invited to take up either one of two options: To take a homestead of 160 acres for each male member of 21 years or over, or to agree to the establishment of a reservation, thus relinquishing all their land in exchange for an indeterminate amount of land as a reservation. If they agreed to accept a reservation, they were promised "a church, a school, and an Indian agent."

Delegate Paul Williams, who also acted as interpreter for the group, made the point that the natives could not be restricted to 160 acres, because their livelihood is made by fishing, hunting, and trapping, and "they have to travel far to do this." The natives also objected to moving away from their villages and homes. The Indians felt strongly opposed to reservations. During the meeting, the chiefs asked again and again that they be informed of laws *in writing* by the United States Government, since they had to rely upon "rumors" for information, and no consideration had been given them as to informing them of laws passed or being considered. At this meeting, the policy of the United States government was expressed. Congressman James Wickersham stated:

"Mr. Riggs is going to build a railroad and these gentlemen are going to continue to survey these lands, and when Mr. Riggs' railroad is built, the white people are going to come in here in great numbers, and push, and push, until the Indians are clear off the best land." Clearly, the government had no intention of protecting Indian land rights, but was attempting to find a way to avoid difficulties with the white settlers, in driving the Indians off their land so that they would be "out of the way" when the white settlers arrived.

Finally, Chief Joe, of Salchoket, summed up the desire of the native people, when he stated: "We want to be left alone." Generally, the Tanana natives wanted these three things: a school, a doctor, and a chance to work.

April 27, 1915: The Territorial Act of 1915 provided a method whereby a nonallotted native could secure a "certificate of citizenship." This procedure involved proof of his general qualifications as a voter, his total abandonment of tribal customs, and his adoption of the culture of civilization. This statute (C 24 Laws of Alaska 1915) became obsolete with the passage of the Citizenship Act (Act of June 2, 1924 c. 233, 43 Stat. 253), which also applied to Alaska natives. The 1915 Act was repealed only in 1933 (C 34 Laws of Alaska, 1933 p. 73). This lapse in defining the rights of the Alaskan natives led to confusion and litigation (Case of U.S. vs Lynch, 1927).

1917: Alaskan natives again see an invasion of white prospectors searching for strategic minerals, as a result of World War 1.

1918: Native villages are decimated by influenza epidemic. Bureau of Indian Affairs establishes three orphanages at Eklutna, Kanakanak (Bristol Bay) and White Mountain (Seward Peninsula) to take care of the children left homeless by the mass deaths of adults.

1920: The Navy cadet training vessel, *The Boxer,* transferred to the Department of the Interior and used as a supply ship for the native villages. Some native villagers were trained on this ship, becoming skilled workers in many capacities. But due to the lack of formal education in scientific subjects, their progress was hampered, and they received no professional certification or status.

1923: The United States Navy and the Department of the Interior assign the Arctic Slope of Alaska to "Petroleum Reserve Number 4." (Hereafter to be known as "Pet #4"). This area is approximately one-twelfth of Alaska's land area. The Slope lies to the north of the Central Plateau, separated from the Plateau by the Brooks Range. Assignment of the Arctic Slope to this Reserve meant that it could not be utilized by any agency, individual, business, or native group other than the U.S. government itself, or by special permission of the government.

July 25, 1923: Sunset Magazine in California receives a letter from an Indian of Kasaan, Alaska, which reveals the plight of the Alaskan people during these years more eloquently than any legal evidence could do. This letter deserves a place in the Chronology:

"When the U.S.A. bought Alaska, the first flag I ever saw was the Stars and Stripes and we Indians were very proud to have the Boston man flag over us. In 1876 there was some gold strike in Alaska which brought many white men to Alaska. Dancing was teached by some of the white men and our Indian women soon became a money making for the dance house keepers, (white men). These dance houses was hell on earth, and soon wiped out the Indian women of Southeastern Alaska. Now there are few Indians in Alaska and these few are at the mercy of the white men who are starving us out. Even the islands where we trap for furs in the winter and picked wild berries for our winter use is taken away from us and made into a fox farm, and we are told if we set foot on these islands we would be shot down like dogs. Our islands are now fox reserves!

"As I said, I don't know how long we Indians lived in Alaska. It's too far away. But one thing I know, we always had salmon enough to eat, and just ten times more Indians to eat them. Yet we had plenty salmon. Big cannery packers are in Alaska now, and they got great big fish trap working in all the waters outside the salmon streams. These traps start from shores by means of nets, stretch out to sea, where piles are driven and a big net bag is placed into which the fish swims. Once in these big bags the fish cannot swim out. The fish is caught now.

"There is no fish can swim past these traps. And this year there is more traps and these traps fish night and day until the season is over. The streams are running, waiting for the salmon. So is the Indian with wife and children on the banks of these streams waiting for his salmon. But there is no salmon to eat. The fish traps got all our fish. These fish trap owners are not hungry. But I am hungry. My people the Indians are hungry. Our babies have no more milk. These big cannery don't know we are hungry, because they are not hungry.

"I wonder why the U.S.A. lets turks own these big canneries, for they are driving us to starvation. These statements is the truth. nothing but the truth so help my God." (*)

Samuel G. Davis, Kasaan, Alaska

1930: Statistical reports reveal that the average annual income of an Eskimo family is between $300-$500. Having replaced by force the satisfying subsistence economy of the native peoples, and thrust the population into an economy based on money, the Eskimos, Aleuts and Indians were left to flounder in poverty. To gain food, one needed money. To gain money, one needed work. There was no work for the native of Alaska.

1930: Alaska Division of the Bureau of Education turns over administration of the reindeer business to the Governor of the state.

March 16, 1931: From 1884 to this date, a Bureau of Education controlled native education, as well as welfare work. On this date, administration of education was turned over to the Bureau of Indian Affairs, which then organized the Alaska Native Service (ANS).

1933: When Harold Ickes is appointed Secretary of the Interior, John Collier becomes Commissioner of Indian Affairs. Collier's administration, which ended in 1945, financed anthropologists to collect and publish the ancient legends of the people, issued a new directory of the rapidly vanishing language of the Aleuts, but failed to improve either their education or their economy; set up an arts and crafts board to promote the sale of Indian and Eskimo handicrafts; and attempted to establish large reservations in both north and south Alaska. The Alaska natives, unlike the Indians of the Lower-Forty-Eight, had never signed any treaties with the United States, nor been allocated definite reserves. Native Alaskans turned down the proposal for establishing reservations. The proposed reservations would have set aside 480,000 acres near Barrow, and 1,472,000 acres around Shugnak.

(*) Original letter by courtesy of the American Indian Historical Society, Indian Library & Archives.

1934: "Eskimos" are designated as "Indians" for the sake of verbal expediency, in the United States law, and in Acts passed by Congress. The term "Indians" as used to include the Eskimo people, has been brought about through certain statutory provisions, and some of these are:

Sec. 19 of the Act of June 18, 1934 (48 Stat. 984,988), providing that: "For the purposes of this Act, Eskimos and other aboriginal peoples of Alaska shall be considered Indians."

Sec. 2 of the Act of April 16, 1934 (48 Stat. 594,596), which grants fishing privileges to "native Indians," defines "native Indians" to mean "members of the aboriginal races inhabiting Alaska when annexed to the United States, and their descendants of the whole or half blood." The term "Indian" is similarly defined in section 142 of the Act of March 3, 1899 (30 Stat. 1253,1274).

1937: The tuberculosis rate among the Eskimos increases to 25 percent of their population.

1939: The U.S. government buys out the Lomen Company reindeer business, as well as all others including those owned by the Laplanders and the Missions. The reindeer industry, however, continues to decline. Reasons are: Herding was not known nor practiced by the Eskimos. Conditions in Alaska were not favorable for "open herding," Eskimo techniques, and the industry requires year-round management, which is entirely incompatible with hunting, fishing, and trapping. These three latter industries constituted the basic economy of the Eskimos. To follow the first meant to abandon the latter. To abandon the latter entirely meant to abandon all hope of future livelihood which meant security for the Eskimos before and during the beginnings of European contact. When little proceeds resulted from the reindeer herding business, Eskimos were forced to seek their old economic life. What transpired can best be described as a vicious circle in which the Eskimo was ensnared and held in a continuing state of impending starvation.

1940-1953: The salmon runs continue to decrease, due to the large fisheries operating in Alaska by absentee owners in San Francisco and Seattle.

1944: The Nome Skin Sewers Cooperative and the Native Ivory Carvers sold about $200,000 worth of goods to the Armed Forces. Migration from outlying villages begins in earnest, to Nome, Anchorage and Fairbanks, and other places where military personnel and operations provide jobs and some economic possibilities. The Navy tests "Pet #4" and reports 100 million-barrel potential, but costs are too high for further studies, or development.

1945: Two Eskimos, one from Nome and one from Wales, are elected to the Territorial House of Representatives.

1946: Military surplus buildings at Seward and Sitka are made into tuberculosis sanatoria.

1955: The Department of the Interior's "Farran Report" exposes the abject poverty, disease, and neglect of Alaska's Natives.

1958: A congressional investigating committee criticizes the Bureau of Indian Affairs' operation of the Wheeler-Howard revolving loan fund for failure to establish any program "in the schools, on the job, or otherwise to train Indians and Eskimos to assume responsible positions in what was supposed to be their own business undertakings," and it had failed "to carry out the Wheeler-Howard Acts' objective of fostering the broadening and diversification of the Indian and Eskimo economic base."

1958: American, Canadian and Russian scholars hold a "Circumpolar Conference" in Copenhagen, to study Arctic archaeology, pool information and arrange for further scientific study.

1959: Alaska acquires statehood, becoming the 49th state of the union. One hundred two million acres of government land was to be given over to the new state. The native leaders, however, disagreed with this proposal and stated that this amounted to a good piece of *native* land, which the United States had no right to dispose of.

1962: The native movement receives a tremendous impetus when *The Tundra Times* is founded. This is the only native newspaper in the state, published weekly, and providing the only source of native communication in Alaska.

1964-67: The state of Alaska leases a total of 900,000 acres of North Slope to Atlantic, Richfield, Humble and Sinclair oil companies.

1964: Tyonek Indians get 12 million dollars from the sale of oil exploration rights.

1966: The Alaska Federation of Natives is founded. The "Land Freeze" is instituted, enacted by Secretary of the Interior Stewart Udall. Alaska's Governor Hickel sues Udall in Alaska's U.S. District Court in an attempt to lift the Freeze, which prevents disposition of land and resources claimed by natives until their claims are settled. Alaska court rules in favor of the state, but the Ninth Circuit Court in San Francisco reverses the decision. At this date, early in 1971, the Land Freeze is still in effect. It is generally agreed by congressmen that no disposition of land or resources may be made until the native land claims are settled.

1966: Natives of Alaska file claim to most of the state of Alaska on the basis of aboriginal rights. More than 372 million acres are claimed as native property. The white Alaskans, especially the attorneys for the state and the oil companies, begin to feel somewhat uneasy as to whether the expected oil boom will actually make them and their constituents instantly rich. Atlantic and Richfield oil companies merge, and together with Humble Oil Company, make tests on Prudhoe Bay.

1968: Atlantic, Richfield, and Humble Oil strike large oil deposits on Prudhoe Bay. The two companies, plus British Petroleum Company, form TAPS (Trans-Alaska Pipeline System). Federal Field committee for Development Planning in Alaska is assigned the job of studying native claims, population, and cultural history. The 565-page report legitimizing native land claim is the result.

1970: The Senate Interior Committee submits a Bill for settlement of the native land claims. Five hundred million dollars is offered, and 2 percent royalties on Alaskan minerals located on public lands not patented to the state, plus four million acres of land. Natives reject the proposal, and claim the amount of land offered is too small as opposed to the claims of 1967. The Bill had no detailed provisions for the organization of Native Development corporations, they stated.

November 25, 1970: An editorial in *The Tundra Times* states the case in connection with the Native Land Claim:

"The Eskimo came to this uninhabited and barren land 30,000 years ago. It was they who discovered it. The Russians only found the land that had been discovered. Hence, it was not their moral right to sell it, nor ours to purchase. This was but a felony compounded . . . The 'Bill of Sale' from Russia is null and void . . . An honest and righteous solution would be to relinquish our ill-advised procurement back to the native . . . A Nation to be truly great must perforce be truly honest."

It is a safe prediction that within the next two years a Chronological Outline History of the Natives of Alaska would more than double the content of this outline. Events are moving rapidly, and the native peoples are now divided as to what must be done to safeguard the future of their children and indeed the future of the whole continent. Alaska today may well be the final step in ecological disaster for North America. Once the Alaskan oil pipeline is built, there is no turning back.

Meanwhile, the economic deprivation of the native continues. Health conditions are no better, despite the enormous expenditures of funds. According to the Report of the Senate Subcommittee on Indian Education, published in 1969, "More Alaskan Natives are unemployed or seasonally employed than have permanent jobs. More than half of the working force is jobless most of the year. Alaska Natives live only half as long as the average American. Native housing in Alaska's villages is generally considered to be the most primitive, dilapidated and substandard housing anywhere in the United States. In most villages, primitive and unsanitary water supply and waste disposal practices have deleterious consequences on native health. . . . The human waste and misery reflected in the preceding pages (of the Report) is a tragedy of major proportions."

In the light of this chronicle of human misery, lack of understanding, misconception and misinterpretation of the true life, history and spirit of the Native Alaskans, we ask again: *Give or Take a Century,* how much longer must we wait for some relief from the degradation and destruction which has been wrought upon us? Perhaps this Chronology should end on a note of warning, issued by a distinguished scholar who wrote, not too long ago:

"Bering Strait is only fifty miles wide; from the mountainside of Wales you can see across it and view East Cape on the Soviet shore. To the Eskimos it has never been a barrier, but a highway uniting kindred on one side with kindred on the other. Two thousand years ago it was bringing from far-eastern Asia new ideas about life and death — techniques to help the living Eskimos hunt the big bowhead whales, and burial rituals that would assist their dead. Before and after Vitus Bering explored the strait that bears his name, or Captain James Cook anchored within it and looked north into the unknown Chukchi Sea, Eskimos from the Asiatic shore were crossing from East Cape to attend the annual trade fair in Kotzebue Sound, where they sold "turquoise" beads and scraps of iron to their American cousins, and initiated them into the joys of tobacco and pipe-smoking.

"Today Bering Strait is still a highway, although the traffic may be temporarily suspended. When it reopens, will it bring to Alaska's Eskimos more modern ideas — concerning the blessings of national socialism perhaps, and the weaknesses of a capitalist system that can leave unfinished, on Alaska's under-developed coast, a task that national socialism might have brought to a speedy conclusion?"

INVENTIONS AND CONTRIBUTIONS

Very little is now known of many perishable items that may have been distinctly Alaskan Native original inventions, and were in use in prehistoric times. Examples are two objects made of ivory and called by anthropologists the *Tridents, Winged Objects, Other Objects,* and *Butterfly Shapes.* These recurring artifacts, made of carved ivory in elaborate shapes, appear to have been made to fit some sort of wooden shaft or handle. Their specific use is still unknown.

A brief resume of the inventions and household items created by the Natives of Alaska, may be given here:

The harpoon, with harpoon head in two variations (Eskimo) (1) The ice hunting harpoon with a fixed shaft and foreshaft, but movable harpoon head; (2) the Kayak harpoon with movable foreshaft and movable harpoon head.

The skinboat or umiak (Eskimo).

The Aleut skinboat or baidarka (Aleut).

The Tlingit dugout canoe (Indian).

The kayak (Eskimo).

Whale bone runners on sleds, sledges and umiaks (Eskimo).

Eskimo dog sled.

The toboggan (Athabascan).

The snow shoe (Indian and Eskimo).

Ice crampons (Eskimo).

Ice testing staffs (Eskimo).

The adze (Eskimo, Indian, Aleut).

The seal net (Eskimo).

Mukluks (Eskimo).

The parka (Eskimo).
The seal oil stone lamp (Eskimo).
Skin scrapers (Eskimo, Indian, Aleut).
The inflated seal skin float (Eskimo).
Tanning of walrus hides in sea water (Eskimo, Aleut).
The cold air trap in entrances to Eskimo houses.
The baleen and seal blubber wolf killer (Eskimo).
Bone needles for sewing (Eskimo, Indian, Aleut).
Baleen baskets (Eskimo).
Eskimo drum.
Methods of storing foods.
Methods of freezing foods, drying foods, smoking.
Extraction of oil from various mammals and fish.
Methods of carving ivory, and bone.
Manufacture of nets, snares, and various other types of fishing technology, invented and used by all the Natives.

Adaptations made following European contact by Eskimos on tools and other items:

Steel blades on harpoon heads, steel points on ice chisels, steel runners on sledges and sleds, steel blades on adzes, iron bits for bow drills, steel blades for knives and ulus.

The most recently recognized contributions made by Eskimos have been in the design and use of cold weather clothing for expeditions and Arctic use. No other man-made materials have excelled the properties of the old-style Eskimo clothing. The Eskimo parka, with its loose-fitting design and wide, roomy bottom hem does two things: It allows for air circulation and keeps an insulating layer of air between the elements and the body. Many outfitters of expeditions have emulated this design and one in Washington state has even patented it as their original down-filled brainstorm!

The same is true of the mukluks. The Eskimo mukluks are usually made with a crimped oogruk hide sole and seal skin uppers. Between the sole and uppers is a thin strip of very flexible, thin seal skin which acts both as a decoration and as a buffer between the extra hard sole and the soft upper. Ample room is allowed for some sort of an insole; in pre-white contact days it was dried grass. The modern insole is usually made of heavy felt.

The U.S. Army's arctic clothing and mukluks are inadequate copies of the parka and the Eskimo mukluk. They are made loosely and of heavy materials. The Eskimo originals are comfortable and light. Any footwear made of so-called insulated rubber is shortly disregarded as cold weather boots by anyone who has ever owned a pair of well-made Eskimo mukluks. The rubberized material holds in body heat to a point where perspiration collects and becomes moisture which then displaces insulating air.

Parka hood ruffs are made of wolverine fur for a reason. Wolverine hair is partly hollow, and it does not collect vaporized air from the breath as easily as other furs do. It is hard in texture and long wearing.

The arts of the Eskimo, Tlingits and Aleuts are some of the most unique and colorful in the world. Decorative motifs used on clothing, decorated skins, carvings, and even the decorations found on ordinary utensils, have fascinated the art expert for a hundred years. The dance as an art is particularly unique, and should be maintained as closely as possible to the original. In music, poetry, ritual observances, the Alaskan Native has much to teach the world of art.

NATIVE ORGANIZATIONS

THE ESKIMO HOUSE, Nome headquarters for four Native Arts Groups: Northwest Skin Sewers Cooperative, Nome; Sunarit Associates Co-op, King Island Villagers, Nome; Ki-Kit-A-Meut Arts and Crafts Co-op, Shishmaref; and Inupiat Arts and Crafts Inc., Teller. Nome.

ANCHORAGE NATIVE WELCOME CENTER, INC., Paul Tiulana, Executive Director, Anchorage.

THE ALEUT LEAGUE (Aleutian Islands, Pribolof Islands and that part of the Alaska Peninsula which is in the Aleutian League).

FAIRBANKS NATIVE WELCOME CENTER, Mrs. Clara Carroll, Director, Fairbanks.

TYONEK, or MOQUAWKI RESERVATION, Emil McCord, Business Council, Tyonek Management Corporation, Koloa Bldg., 1675 "C" Street, Anchorage.

TANANA CHIEFS CONFERENCE, Alfred Ketzler, President, Tanana.

BERING STRAITS ASSOCIATION (Seward Peninsula, Unalakleet, St. Lawrence Island).

NORTHWEST ALASKA NATIVE ASSOCIATION, Robert Newlin, President, Kotzebue.

ASSOCIATION OF VILLAGE COUNCIL PRESIDENTS (Southwest Coast, All villages on the Bethel area, including all villages on the Lower Yukon River and the Lower Kuskokwim River).

COOK INLET NATIVE ASSOCIATION (CINA), Kenai, Tyonek, Eklutna, and Illiamna.

BRISTOL BAY NATIVE ASSOCIATION (Dillingham, Upper Alaska Peninsula).
CHUGACH NATIVE ASSOCIATION, Gilbert Olsen, President (Cordova, Tatitlek, Port Graham, English Bay, Valdez and Seward).
KODIAK AREA NATIVE ASSOCIATION (All villages on and around Kodiak Island).
COPPER RIVER NATIVE ASSOCIATION (Copper Center, Glennallen, Chitina, and Mentasta).
THE ALEUT COMMUNITY COUNCIL, St. Paul.

Names You Should Know

JACK AHGOOK, DANNY HUGO, MAY KAKINYA, DAVID MEDIANA, AMOS MORRY, ROBERT PANEAK, JOHNNY RULLAND, RILEY SIKUAYAGAK, Eskimos, Concerned Citizens of Anaktuvuk Pass.

JOHN BORBRIDGE, Tlingit, President, Central Council of Tlingit and Haida Indians, Juneau.

EMILY BROWN, Eskimo, Secretary, Alaskan Heritage Writers' Association, College.

WILLIAM DEMMERT, JR., Tlingit-Sioux, Former School principal, Klawock, Ph. D. Candidate in Education, Harvard University.

CHARLES EDWARDSON, Eskimo, President, Friends of Alaska Natives (FAN), Point Barrow.

MARY HALE, Chairman, Alaska State Arts Council, Anchorage.

WILLIE HENSLEY, Eskimo, Alaska State Senator, Kotzebue.

EBEN HOPSON, Eskimo, Executive Director, Alaska Federation of Natives, Kotzebue.

CHIEF ANDREW ISAAC, Athapascan, Tanacross Elder and Native Leader, Tanacross.

JERRY IVEY, Athapascan, PHS Native Affairs Officer, Anchorage.

ADAM JOHN, Athapascan, Anchorage Community College, Native Studies Program Student, Anchorage.

MICHAEL KRAUSS, Athapascan Languages Instructor, University of Alaska, College.

FLORE LEKANOF, Aleut; 1st President of the Aleut League.

BRYON MALLOT, Tlingit, Executive Director, Rural Alaska Community Action Program.

ALFRED NAKAK, Eskimo, Nome Center Director of the Inupiak Development Corporation, Nome.

ROBERT NEWLIN, Eskimo, President, Northwest Alaska Native Association, Kotzebue.

EMIL NOTTI, Athapascan, President AFN (To 1970).

JOHN NUSUNGINYA, Eskimo, Arctic Slope Native Association Board Member, Point Barrow.

FREDERICK PAUL, Tlingit, Attorney for Arctic Slope Native Association.

GABRIEL PAYENNA, Eskimo, Manager, Sunarit Associates, King Island Village, Nome.

CAROL PISCOYA, Eskimo, Manager, Eskimo House, Nome.

IRENE REED, Eskimo Language Workshop, University of Alaska, College.

HOWARD ROCK, Eskimo, Editor of *Tundra Times,* Fairbanks.

PETER SEEGANNA, Eskimo, Assistant Supervisor, Indian Arts and Crafts Board, Nome.

RONALD SENUNGETUK, Eskimo, Professor, Native Arts Program, University of Alaska, College.

JEROME TRIGG, Eskimo, Executive Director, Nome Chapter, Alaska Native Brotherhood, Nome.

JOE UPICKSOUN, Eskimo, President, Arctic Slope Native Association, Point Barrow.

JANE WALLEN, Director, Alaska State Museum, Juneau.

CLIFFORD WEYIONANA, Eskimo, Manager, Ki-Kit-A-Meut Arts and Crafts, Inc., Shishmaref.

DONALD WRIGHT, Eskimo & Athapascan, President (from 1970), AFN, Fairbanks.